LOVE IS TH
EXPLANATIO
OF EVERYTHII

POPE JOHN PAUL II

LOVE IS THE EXPLANATION OF EVERYTHING

365 Meditations with the Pope

Essential Thoughts of Pope John Paul II
on Questions of Faith and Conscience

RIZZOLI
NEW YORK

New York Paris London Milan

First published in the United States of America in 2011 by
Rizzoli International Publications, Inc.
300 Park Avenue South
New York, NY 10010
www.rizzoliusa.com

Originally published in Italian as *L'amore è la spiegazione di tutto* in 2010 by
RCS Libri S.p.A.

2011 2012 2013 2014 / 10 9 8 7 6 5 4 3 2 1

ISBN: 978-0-8478-3670-3

Library of Congress Control Number: 2011923717

The English text reproduced herein has been either provided by the
Vatican or translated from Italian by Antony Shugaar.

Texts selected by Isabella Planelli

Picture research: Studio Bajetta, Isabella Planelli, and
Carla Maria Colombo

Editorial coordination: Studio Bajetta

Graphic design and layout: Davide Vincenti

Production: Sergio Daniotti

Printed in China

To the Lord's question "Karol, do you love me?" the archbishop of Cracow answered from the depths of his heart: "Lord, you know everything; you know that I love you." The love of Christ was the dominant force in the life of our beloved Holy Father. Anyone who ever saw him pray, who ever heard him preach, knows that. Thanks to his being profoundly rooted in Christ, he was able to bear a burden that transcends merely human abilities: to be the shepherd of Christ's flock, of his universal Church.

Homily of His Eminence Cardinal Joseph Ratzinger

Funeral Mass of the Roman Pontiff John Paul II

April 8, 2005

1

Their Eminences the Cardinals have summoned a new bishop of Rome. They summoned him from a distant country – distant, but very close in terms of communion in faith and in the Christian tradition. I was afraid when I received this appointment, but I acted in the spirit of obedience to our Lord Jesus Christ and in total faith in his Mother, the Holy Virgin.

I don't know how well I can express myself in your . . . our Italian language. If I make mistakes, you will correct me. And so I present myself to you all, to confess together our common faith, our hope, our trust in the Mother of Christ and of the Church, as well as to start once again down this path of history and of the Church, with the help of God and the help of men.

FIRST GREETING AND BENEDICTION OF THE FAITHFUL
October 16, 1978

Do not be afraid. Open wide the doors for Christ. To his saving power open the boundaries of states, economic and political systems, the vast fields of culture, civilization, and development. Do not be afraid. Christ knows what is in man. He alone knows it.

So often today man does not know what is within him, in the depths of his mind and heart. So often he is uncertain about the meaning of his life on this earth. He is assailed by doubt, a doubt that turns into despair. We ask you therefore, we beg you with humility and trust, let Christ speak to man. He alone has words of life—yes, of eternal life.

HOMILY FOR THE INAUGURATION OF HIS PONTIFICATE
October 22, 1978

3 And you, dear young people, do you really feel, deeply, that you are the hope and the joyful promise of tomorrow? Certainly, awareness of youthfulness is not sufficient to give the sense of that inner confidence, which alone makes it possible to look to the future with the calm certainty of being able to change the forces operating in the world, for the construction of a society really worthy of man.

To be young means living within oneself an incessant newness of spirit, nourishing a continual quest for good, releasing an impulse to change always for the better, realizing a persevering determination of dedication.

SPEECH TO YOUTH
November 15, 1978

I rejoice with you and I wonder why you have come. Perhaps you came to see if the Pope is at home on the second day of Christmas. And then, I think you have come because today is really a beautiful day and attracts one outside. But the Pope has to stay at home because he never knows when people are coming to recite the Angelus. Then I think you have come because you know that the Pope needs your prayers and needs above all to pray with you. I thank you for this and for this unexpected but certainly all the more welcome and precious presence of yours. I want to wish everyone a Happy Christmas again. Especially the young. . . .

I do not understand what you are saying. You do not have microphones. But I understand that you love the Pope. Thank you and a Merry Christmas to all of you again. Blessed be the name of the Lord.

ANGELUS
December 26, 1978

It is . . . to the oldest that we must look with respect ("honor!"); to them families owe their existence, education, and maintenance, which have often been paid for with hard work and much suffering.

They cannot be treated as if they were now useless. Even if they sometimes lack the strength to be able to carry out the simplest actions, they have, however, experience of life and the wisdom that the young often lack. . . .

Therefore, the Pope's thoughts and prayer go to you old people today. I hope that all those present are willingly in harmony with the Pope; I hope that above all the youngest are. Grandchildren love their grandfathers and their grandmothers, and keep them company better than others.

ANGELUS
December 31, 1978

In spite of all this, the rural world possesses enviable human and religious riches: a deep-rooted love of the family; the sense of friendship; help for the needy; deep humanism; love of peace and civil society; a deep religious sense; trust and opening to God; promotion of love for the Blessed Virgin; and so many others. It is a well-deserved tribute of recognition that the Pope wishes to express to you, and for which society is indebted to you. Thank you, rural workers, for your precious contribution to social good; mankind owes you a great deal.

I think of you, boys and girls, young people of working-class families; there comes into my mind the figure of him who was born in an artisan's family, who grew in age, wisdom, and grace, who learned from his Mother human ways, and who had his teacher in life and in daily work in the just man that God gave him as father. The Church venerates this Mother and this man; this holy worker, model of a man and, at the same time, of a worker.

Our Lord Jesus Christ received the caresses of his strong worker's hands, hands hardened by work, but open to kindness and to needy brothers. Allow me to enter your homes; yes, you want to have the Pope as your guest and friend, and to give him the consolation of seeing in your homes the union and the family love that gives rest, after a hard day's work, in this relationship of mutual affection that reigned in the Holy Family.

The suffering of one's neighbor, the suffering of another man, the same as oneself in everything, always causes a certain uneasiness, almost a sense of embarrassment, in those who are not suffering. A question arises instinctively: why he, and not I? One cannot avoid this question which is the elementary expression of human solidarity. . . .

We must stop, then, in front of suffering, in front of suffering man, to rediscover this essential link between our own human "self" and his. We must stop before suffering man, to testify to him and, as far as possible, together with him, all the dignity of suffering, I would say all the majesty of suffering. We must bow our heads before brothers or sisters who are weak and helpless, deprived of just what has been granted to us to enjoy every day.

ANGELUS
February 11, 1979

Dear Bride and Bridegroom,

You will shortly utter the words of the sacramental promise that will make you husband and wife in Christ Jesus before God and the Church. They are concise words (you certainly know them by heart), but their significance, their special importance, their unitive power, are particularly great. Promising each other love, faithfulness, and virtue in marriage, not only will you confirm again what your young hearts bear witness to now, but at the same time you will lay the foundations for the construction of the home of your common future. Man must live on the earth, and to live there he needs not only a building constructed on a material foundation; today he needs a spiritual foundation. Love, faithfulness, and virtue in marriage constitute that foundation on which alone the matrimonial community can rest, the foundation on which the spiritual dwelling for the future family can be built.

BLESSING AT THE WEDDING OF TWO YOUNG ROMANS
February 25, 1979

The redeemer of man, Jesus Christ, is the center of the universe and of history. To him go my thoughts and my heart in this solemn moment of the world that the Church and the whole family of present-day humanity are now living. In fact, this time . . . is already very close to the year 2000. . . . For the Church, the People of God spread, although unevenly, to the most distant limits of the earth, it will be the year of a great Jubilee. We are already approaching that date, which, without prejudice to all the corrections imposed by chronological exactitude, will recall and reawaken in us in a special way our awareness of the key truth of faith which Saint John expressed at the beginning of his Gospel: "The Word became flesh and made his dwelling among us" (1:14), and elsewhere: "God so loved the world that he gave his only Son, so that everyone who believes in him might not perish but might have eternal life" (3:16).

ENCYCLICAL REDEMPTOR HOMINIS, § 1
March 4, 1979

1

God entered the history of humanity and, as a man, became an actor in that history, one of the thousands of millions of human beings but at the same time unique! Through the Incarnation God gave human life the dimension that he intended man to have from his first beginning; he has granted that dimension definitively—in the way that is peculiar to him alone, in keeping with his eternal love and mercy, with the full freedom of God—and he has granted it also with the bounty that enables us, in considering the original sin and the whole history of the sins of humanity, and in considering the errors of the human intellect, will, and heart, to repeat with amazement the words of the Sacred Liturgy: "O happy fault, which gained us so great a Redeemer!"

ENCYCLICAL REDEMPTOR HOMINIS, § 1
March 4, 1979

We are not dealing with the "abstract" man, but the real, "concrete," "historical" man. We are dealing with "each" man, for each one is included in the mystery of the redemption, and with each one Christ has united himself forever through this mystery. Every man comes into the world through being conceived in his mother's womb and being born of his mother, and precisely on account of the mystery of the redemption is entrusted to the solicitude of the Church. Her solicitude is about the whole man and is focused on him in an altogether special manner. The object of her care is man in his unique unrepeatable human reality, which keeps intact the image and likeness of God himself. . . . Man as "willed" by God, as "chosen" by him from eternity and called, destined for grace and glory – this is "each" man, "the most concrete" man, "the most real"; this is man in all the fullness of the mystery in which he has become a sharer in Jesus Christ, the mystery in which each one of the four thousand million human beings living on our planet has become a sharer from the moment he is conceived beneath the heart of his mother.

ENCYCLICAL REDEMPTOR HOMINIS, § 13
March 4, 1979

Emigration is a massive phenomenon of our time, a permanent phenomenon, which is even assuming new forms, and which concerns all continents, and nearly all countries. It raises serious human and spiritual problems. It is a test, that is, a risk and a chance, for the immigrants and for those who receive them. Yes, it involves for the former a serious risk of uprooting, dehumanization, and, in some cases, of dechristianization; for the latter a risk of rejecting, of stiffening. But it also implies a chance of human and spiritual enrichment, opening, welcoming of foreigners, and mutual renewal thanks to this contact. And for the Church, it is an invitation to be more missionary, to go to meet the foreign brother, to respect him, to bear witness, in this context, to her faith and her charity, and to accept the other's positive contribution.

SPEECH TO THE WORLD CONGRESS ON MIGRATION, ROME, ITALY
March 15, 1979

14

Modern man experiences the threat of spiritual indifference and even of the death of conscience; and this death is something deeper than sin: it is the killing of the sense of sin. Today so many factors contribute to killing conscience in the men of our time, and this corresponds to that reality that Christ called "sin against the Holy Spirit." This sin begins when the word of the Cross no longer speaks to man as the last cry of love, which has the power of rending hearts. "Scindite corda vestra."

The Church does not cease to pray for the conversion of sinners, for the conversion of every man, of each of us, precisely because she respects, because she esteems, man's greatness and depth and rereads the mystery of his heart through the mystery of Christ.

My sons and daughters, you have pointed out at your Congress the sufferings and the contradictions by which a society is seen to be overwhelmed when it moves away from God. The wisdom of Christ makes you capable of pushing on to discover the deepest source of evil existing in the world. And it also stimulates you to proclaim to all men, your companions in study today, and in work tomorrow, the truth you have learned from the Master's lips, that is, that evil comes "from within people, from their hearts" (Mk 7:21). . . . The root of evil is within man. The remedy, therefore, also starts from the heart.

It is here that the Lord wishes to lead us: within ourselves. All this time that precedes Easter is a constant call to conversion of the heart.

Beloved sons and daughters, have, therefore, the courage to repent; and have also the courage to draw God's grace from sacramental Confession. This will make you free!

SPEECH TO UNIVERSITY STUDENTS, ROME, ITALY
April 10, 1979

The Good Shepherd is Jesus Christ, the Son of God and of Mary, our brother and Redeemer; it must be said, in fact, that he is the only, true and eternal shepherd of our souls! While he attributes this title to himself, he takes care to justify the reason and the validity of this personal attribution: only he, in fact, knows his sheep and they know him (cf. Jn 10:14); only he "lays down his life for the sheep" (Jn 10:11); only he guides them and leads them along safe ways; only he defends them from evil, symbolized by the rapacious wolf.

In this wonderful work, however, Christ does not want to be and to act alone, but he intends to associate with himself collaborators – men chosen among men in favor of other men (cf. Heb 5:1). These he calls with a special "vocation" of love, invests with his sacred powers and sends as apostles into the world, so that they may continue his salvific mission, always and everywhere, until the end of time. Christ, therefore, needs, wills to need, the response, the zeal, the love of those who are "called," so that he may still know, guide, defend, and love so many other sheep, sacrificing also life for them, if necessary!

ANGELUS
May 6, 1979

17

Motherhood must be treated in work policy and economy as a great end and a great task in itself. For with it is connected the mother's work in giving birth, feeding, and rearing, and no one can take her place. Nothing can take the place of the heart of a mother always present and always waiting in the home. True respect for work brings with it due esteem for motherhood. It cannot be otherwise. The moral health of the whole of society depends on that.

HOLY MASS FOR WORKERS AT JASNA GÓRA, CZĘSTOCHOWA, POLAND
June 6, 1979

Get to know Christ and make yourselves known to him. He knows each one of you in a particular way. It is not a knowledge that arouses opposition and rebellion, a knowledge that forces one to flee in order to safeguard his own inward mystery. It is not a knowledge made up of hypotheses and reducing man to his dimensions of social utility. The knowledge of Christ is a knowledge full of the simple truth about "man" and, above all, full of love. Submit yourselves to this simple and loving knowledge of the Good Shepherd. Be certain that he knows each one of you more than each one of you knows himself. He knows because he has laid down his life (cf. Jn 15:13).

Allow him to find you. A human being, a young person, at times gets lost in himself, in the world about him, and in all the network of human affairs that wrap him round. Allow Christ to find you. Let him know all about you and guide you.

MEETING WITH UNIVERSITY STUDENTS, CRACOW, POLAND
June 8, 1979

It is to you, boys and girls, who spend your childhood serenely in closeness with the Holy Virgin, that I address my affectionate and paternal greetings. You know how much Jesus loves little children! Children, fascinated by his words and his personality, exuberantly manifested their fondness for him; and Jesus wanted to be with children, he would not allow his apostles to keep them away from him: "Let the children come to me and do not prevent them," he said, "for the kingdom of God belongs to such as these" (Lk 18:16). The Pope, too, like Jesus, loves you very much, trusts in your prayers, and today, in this meeting, tells you: Always be sincere and faithful friends of Jesus; study his examples, his life, his teachings, contained in the Holy Gospel. But being sincere and faithful friends of Jesus means following him, putting into practice, every day, the things that he said. Then you will be truly happy, because you will be exemplary Christians and good citizens.

SPEECH AT THE SANCTUARY OF THE BLESSED VIRGIN OF THE ROSARY, POMPEII, ITALY
October 21, 1979

A human created by God and elevated by him to the sublime dignity of being his son carries within himself an irrepressible aspiration to happiness and feels a natural aversion for all kinds of suffering. Jesus, in contrast, in the course of his evangelizing, while stooping to heal and comfort the sick and the suffering, never avoided suffering itself, but chose instead to subject himself to as much human pain as possible, both moral and physical, in his Passion up to and including the mortal agony in Gethsemane, his abandonment by his Father on Calvary, his long agony, and his Death on the Cross. That is why he said that blessed are they who mourn and they who hunger and thirst for righteousness.

SPEECH TO THE SICK, POMPEII, ITALY
October 21, 1979

I know that you devote a great deal of time to play. Well, you must know that play is not merely a matter of carefree amusement but, even when you do not realize it, an important occasion for education and virtue. In the life that lies ahead of you, you will also be asked to work with and even measure yourself against other people, in dealing with problems, situations, and projects that, in fact, make life very much like a game to be played honestly; that game involves the intelligent use of one's resources, a clear understanding of the general context in which one is operating, the ability to adapt oneself to the pace of others, and a fair and generous sense of competition. That is why there is no clear distinction between school and play: they both help to build your personality because they both have a great deal to teach you, and they are both expressions of a youth that is not only external but internal as well.

SPEECH TO STUDENTS, ROME, ITALY
March 1, 1980

Love is the explanation of everything. A love that opens up to the other person in his unique individuality and speaks the decisive words: "I want you to be there." Unless we begin with this acceptance of the other, however he may appear, recognizing in him a true if perhaps indistinct image of Christ, we cannot say that we truly love. All authentic love recapitulates to a certain degree the original evaluation of God, as we repeat with the Creator, with respect to every single human being, that his existence is "very good" (Gn 1:31).

PASTORAL VISIT TO COTTOLENGO, TURIN, ITALY
April 13, 1980

"Do you love?" A fundamental question, a common question. It is the question that opens the heart—and that gives meaning to life. It is the question that determines the true dimension of a human being. In it, the whole person is summoned to express himself and to go beyond himself as well.

"Do you love me?" Here, in this place, during our first meeting, this question had to be posed: "Do you love me?" But it must be posed always and everywhere. This question is asked of man by God. This question man must continually ask himself.

Christ asked Peter this question. Christ asked three times, and three times Peter answered him. "Simon, son of John, do you love me? Yes, Lord, you know that I love you" (Jn 21:15–17).

HOLY MASS, NÔTRE DAME, PARIS, FRANCE
May 30, 1980

The calling of each of us merges, up to a certain point, with our very being: we might say that the calling and the person become the same thing. This means that in God's creative initiative there enters a particular act of love for those called, not only to salvation, but also to the ministry of salvation. Therefore throughout eternity, since we first began to exist in the plans of the Creator, he chose to call us as well, predisposing in us the gifts and the conditions for a conscious and personal response to the summons of Christ and of the Church. God who loves us, who is love, is also "he who calls."

Therefore, in the face of a calling, let us worship the mystery, let us respond with love to the initiative of love, let us say yes to the summons.

SPEECH TO FUTURE PRIESTS, PÔRTO ALEGRE, BRAZIL
July 5, 1980

I do everything possible to meet everyone: rich and poor; those who live in comfort, or at least relative comfort; and those who face great challenges in making a living. To everyone, I wish to speak and testify to the love of our Lord Jesus Christ, that they may believe in him and that they may attain salvation.

But those who are less blessed with worldly goods, because they have greater need of help and consolation, always occupy a special place in my concern to ensure that I am faithfully carrying on Christ's mission: "Bring glad tidings to the poor," the salvation of God.

VISIT TO ALAGADOS, THE FAVELAS OF SALVADOR DA BAHIA, BRAZIL
July 7, 1980

Young people, to you I say: do your best to unite your efforts to ensure this joy to yourselves and to those whom you meet on your daily path, in your family, at school, at work, and at play. There are young people like yourselves who have not yet found this joy, there are busy men and women who cannot find the time to seek it, there are sick people in hospitals and old people in nursing homes and hospices who are suffering because they are lonely and abandoned. All these brothers and sisters await only a smile from you, a word from you, your help, your friendship, and the clasp of your hand.

Deny no one the joy that comes from such deeds: you will thus bring comfort to them and well-being to yourself, because, as the Sacred Scriptures tell us, "It is more blessed to give than to receive" (Acts 20:35).

SPEECH TO YOUTH, SIENA, ITALY
September 14, 1980

Libertad, the name of the school ship in which you ply the seas and visit many nations, is a permanent invitation to shape your lives in keeping with the criteria of liberty of the children of God. Saint Paul states that Christian liberty is total, but only insofar as one is guided by a sense of responsibility toward one's neighbor and oneself, thus serving God. Only liberty understood in this way makes the construction of peace possible.

The Church makes every effort to assure that this society to which you belong respects the dignity, the liberty, and the rights of people, and you too are those individuals. In the name of Christ I exhort you to expand your hearts to encompass the world and to put your energies at the service of your brothers. Be generous and sincere. Contribute to the building of a better world where peace reigns always, the fruit of liberty, love, and justice.

GREETING TO ARGENTINE CADETS, CASTEL GANDOLFO, ITALY
September 19, 1980

We are all runners in a sense, as Saint Basil the Great reminds us, each of us moving quickly toward our destination.

"You are placed as a traveler in this life; you pass by all things, and everything is left behind you. You saw a plant or grass or water on the way, or any other worthwhile sight. You enjoyed it a little, then you passed on. Again, you came upon stones, gullies, peaks, cliffs, and palisades, or perhaps, even wild beasts, reptiles, thorns, and other troublesome objects; you were a little distressed, then you left them behind" (Saint Basil, *On Psalm 1*, § 4).

A crystalline Christian faith . . . will give serenity to your life and will serve as a clear example to those who know you: "Just so, your light must shine before others, that they may see your good deeds and glorify your heavenly Father," Jesus told us in the Sermon on the Mount (Mt 5:16).

SPEECH TO ITALIAN RAILROAD WORKERS ON PILGRIMAGE
October 26, 1980

Work is human effort. It is the conscious and personal pursuit of man—his contribution to the great undertaking of generations, the activity involved in the sustenance and progress of humanity, of nations, and of families. It is clear that men occupied in a given kind of work have the right to associate freely for the purposes of that work, in order to obtain all the benefits that work is intended to serve. This is one of the fundamental human rights, the right of man as worker, who, "subduing the earth" (to use the biblical term) precisely by his labor, desires that both in the workplace and in labor matters, human life on this earth should become truly humane, and indeed increasingly humane (as we read, for instance, in the texts of the last Council).

SPEECH TO A DELEGATION OF THE POLISH LABOR UNION SOLIDARITY
January 5, 1981

Our response to God's gift is made with human effort and work. . . . I feel deep joy when I meet workers like you, for you remind me of those years in my youth when I too experienced the grandeur and severity, the happy hours and the moments of anxiety, the achievements and the frustrations that a worker's condition entails. . . . You know the dignity and the nobility of your work — you who work to live, to improve your life, to provide for your children's sustenance, education, and well-being. Your work is noble because it is a service for your families and for the wider community that is society. Work is a service in which man himself grows to the extent to which he gives himself for others.

HOLY MASS FOR FARMERS, LEGAZPI CITY, PHILIPPINES
February 21, 1981

You have also submitted questions for me about music. I do not play any musical instrument. I've never actively devoted myself to this artistic field. But I deeply appreciate the beauty of music and I very much like to sing. I have spent many hours (especially during the holidays) singing with young people. And even now, during the holidays, various youth groups come to Castel Gandolfo and sing. I cherish the hope that one day you too will come . . . even though I know that it's a very long way!

As for different kinds of music, I seem to appreciate particularly deeply the beauty of liturgical music (Gregorian chants!), but I also love contemporary music: Gershwin, for instance, Louis Armstrong, Taki Rentaro, Toshiro Mayuzumi, and others. Of course, Chopin and Szymanowski are close to my heart, but I also love Beethoven, Bach, and Mozart.

SPEECH TO YOUTH, TOKYO, JAPAN
February 24, 1981

It is with deep emotion that I greet all those who still bear upon their bodies the marks of the destruction that was visited upon them the day of that unforgettable explosion. The sufferings you have undergone have also inflicted a wound in the heart of every human being on earth. Your lives here today are the most persuasive appeal that could be made to all men of goodwill, the most convincing argument against war and in favor of peace. I am reminded in this moment of the words spoken by the mayor of Hiroshima two years after the first nuclear explosion: "For only those who most bitterly experienced and came to know most completely the misery and the guilt of war can utterly reject war as the most terrible kind of human suffering, and ardently pursue peace." We are all in your debt because you are a constant, living appeal for peace.

MEETING WITH ATOMIC BOMB VICTIMS, HILL OF MERCY HOSPITAL, NAGASAKI, JAPAN
February 26, 1981

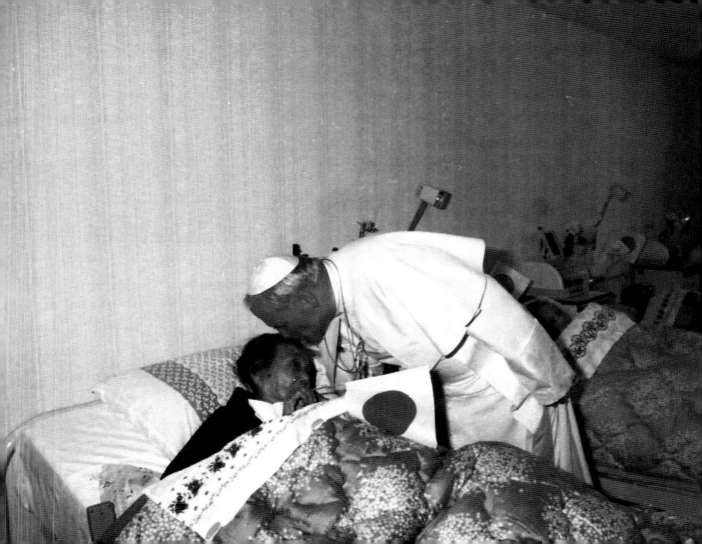

With the Gospels, art entered history. From the small towns of Galilee and Judea, people gathered to hear the message. And Jesus performed a magnificent transformation, he cast the stories, as we might put it in modern terms, in such a manner that they could be seen as well as heard. He spoke of the shepherd who had lost his sheep, of the sower who sowed his seeds in different soils, and the prodigal son who left home. And the listeners immediately understood that the stories were about them, lost sheep, seeds that should have sprouted, sons sought after by the love of their Father.

SPEECH TO THE ITALIAN NATIONAL CONFERENCE FOR SACRED ART
April 27, 1981

"And behold, I am with you always, until the end of the age" (Mt 28:20). This promise that, paradoxically, Jesus made to his disciples at the very moment in which he was leaving them was kept in a singular manner in the Sacrament of the Eucharist. Under the palpable signs of the bread and the wine, Jesus becomes present at a certain time and place, allowing every human being, wherever they might be and in whatever historic epoch they might live, to establish a personal contact with him. Jesus chose to remain close to us, not merely to console us in our daily trials and to help us to accept life with its burden of misfortunes, injustices, and abuses. He is also near us in order to sustain us in our struggle against all manifestations of evil on earth and to encourage us in our commitment to making history progress toward goals more worthy of humanity.

ANGELUS
July 19, 1981

Work is collaboration with God in the perfection of nature, in keeping with the biblical precept to subdue the earth. The Creator wanted man to be explorer, conqueror, and ruler of the land and the seas, of their treasures, their energies, and their secrets, in order that man might regain his true greatness as the "partner of God." That is why work is noble and sacred: it is the title of human sovereignty over Creation. Work, moreover, is a means of union and solidarity, making all men brothers, teaching them cooperation, strengthening their rapport, and spurring them to the attainment of things, but especially of hope, freedom, and love. Through the functional divisions of production, work can create a conscious and close-knit fabric of collaboration, making society more harmoniously effective in the pursuit of a just order for one and all.

ANGELUS
September 27, 1981

We have a Europe of culture, with the great philosophical, artistic, and religious movements that distinguish it, making it the leader of all continents; we have the Europe of work which, by means of scientific and technological research, has developed through various stages of civilization to arrive at the current age of industry and cybernetics; but there is also the Europe of the tragedies of peoples and nations, the Europe of blood, tears, battles, ruptures, and the most horrifying cruelty. Over Europe, despite the message of the great spirits, the grim and terrible tragedy of sin and evil has been felt, sowing, as in the Gospel parable, the fatal seeds of discord in the fields of history. Nowadays, the problem that confronts us is how to safeguard Europe and the world from further catastrophes!

Europe needs Christ and the Gospels, because in them are the roots of all its peoples. May you too hear this message!

SPEECH ON THE COMMON CHRISTIAN ROOTS OF THE EUROPEAN NATIONS
November 6, 1981

The family comes from God. It is the Creator who has arranged the loving covenant of one man and one woman. He has blessed their love and made it a source of mutual help. He has made it fruitful, and established its permanence until death. In the Creator's plan, the family is a community of persons. Therefore, the fundamental form of life and love within the family lies in respect for each person, for each individual member of the family. Husbands and wives, consider and treat each other with the greatest respect. Parents, respect the unique personality of your children. Children, show your parents obedient respect. All members of the family must feel accepted, and respected, because they must feel loved. In a special way, the old and the sick.

HOLY MASS FOR FAMILIES, ONITSHA, NIGERIA
February 13, 1982

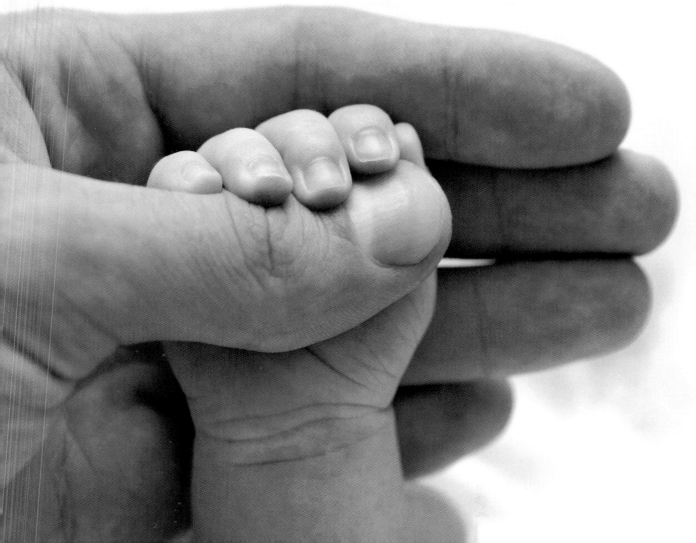

Because it is part of Church tradition to consider Christian everything that is authentically human, I feel it is my duty to advise you with some urgency to increasingly humanize the medicine that you practice and to establish a bond of sincere human solidarity with your patients, above and beyond your purely professional relationship. A person is always a subject and should be approached as such. This is the original dignity of a human being. And it is precisely in our relationship with a suffering man that we find ourselves subjected to a challenge that tests and puts to the proof the existence and authenticity of our convictions on the matter. A person demands by his very nature a personal relationship. Even a patient is never merely a clinical case, but always a "sick man"; he expects competent and effective care, but also the ability and the art of instilling confidence and trust, possibly to the point of discussing honestly with him his condition, and above all the adoption of a sincere attitude of "sympathy," in the etymological sense of the term.

SPEECH TO A MEDICAL CONFERENCE ON TUMOR THERAPY, ROME, ITALY
February 25, 1982

I have come to listen, together with you, to the words, strong and clear, of those who died, victims of the irrational and senseless logic of homicidal barbarity.

Here, where violence was unleashed in all its vast folly, they urge everyone to extend solidarity and understanding, and they assure us that the ultimate victory will be that of love, not of hatred; they warn us that when you deny and offend God, you deny and offend man as well, by diminishing human beings to instruments of one's whims, of one's ideologies, and of one's plans for power and abuse; they ask that their pain and suffering should not be without some use to human society, and that Rome, Italy, Europe, and the world might live in justice, in harmony, in peace, and in a reciprocal respect for the inalienable rights of the human being, created in the image and likeness of God.

Dry the humanly inconsolable tears of their families, who expect and demand truth and justice, and give them the grace of being able to forgive with the strength of Christ Crucified.

Penetrate in the hearts of those who, by tainting themselves with such an inhuman crime, have desecrated and wounded man, created in Your image and likeness.

Open their eyes, blinded and distorted by hatred, that they may understand that a new and better society cannot be built on hatred and scorn, much less on the extermination of one's brothers.

Comfort those who, every day, perform their duty in silence and in secret, thus bringing their precious and meritorious contribution to the spiritual and civil progress of humanity.

Turn Your benevolent gaze on this city, which has had to pay a high price in blood and suffering over these recent years; may it be able to find in its fertile Christian roots the strength to continue with new impetus its progress along the paths of peace, solidarity, and harmony.

PRAYER COMMEMORATING THE RAILROAD STATION BOMBING OF AUGUST 2, 1980, BOLOGNA, ITALY
April 18, 1982

A visit to a hospital, and especially to a children's hospital, provokes in the depths of the heart some of the most radical questions about the meaning of life and the existence of man: the continual, relentless, ineluctable presence of suffering, especially the suffering of the innocent, strikes the astonished and perplexed human mind like a real scandal. The heartfelt lament and piercing cry of a suffering child may almost seem like a protest of all of humanity against the impenetrable silence of a God who allows so much pain.

Where human reason seems to stumble against an opaque wall of shadow, the Divine Word introduces us to the mystery of human suffering, submitting for our consideration and experience Jesus, Christ and Lord, Son of God, in whom we see incarnated the prophetic figure of the suffering Servant, the man of sorrows (Is 53:3); Jesus, who is profoundly moved in the presence of the suffering of others; who completely assumes the pain in his Passion and Death, the obligatory passage for his Resurrection and Glorification.

VISIT TO THE PEDIATRIC HOSPITAL OF THE BABY JESUS, ROME, ITALY
June 8, 1982

Yes, brothers and sisters, we were made for the Lord, who stamped in us the immortal imprint of his power and his love. The great resources of man spring from this, consist in this, and find their safeguarding only in God. The greatness of man lies in his intelligence, through which he is able to know himself, others, the world, and God; the greatness of man lies in his will, whereby he is able to give himself in love, attaining pinnacles of heroism. It is on these resources that the irrepressible aspiration of man is founded: the aspiration toward truth — this is the life of the intelligence — and the aspiration toward freedom — this is the breath of the will. Here man acquires his great, incomparable stature, which no one can crush underfoot, which no one can mock, which no one can deprive him of.

SPEECH TO THE THIRD MEETING FOR FRIENDSHIP AMONG PEOPLES, RIMINI, ITALY
August 29, 1982

You outshine the poverty of our thoughts, feelings, and words; that is why we wish to learn to adore Your mystery in admiration, loving it as it is, speechless with a friendly silence and a giving presence. In our physical and moral nights, if You are present, You love us and You speak to us, even though, in many cases, we do not perceive the consolation. By learning this dimension of adoration, we will stay in Your intimacy or mystery; then our prayer will be converted in respect to the mystery of every brother and every event to introduce into our own family and social setting, and build history with this active and fecund silence that is born of contemplation. Thanks to You, our capacity for silence and adoration will be converted into a capacity for loving and serving.

PRAYER DURING THE NOCTURNAL ADORATION, MADRID, SPAIN
October 31, 1982

It does not escape me that, in the midst of your hard work, at times discouragement may creep in, or the fog may thicken that covers faith. It is then, in particular, that you must be able to rely upon prayer and remember that the Lord will not abandon you, that you were summoned by Jesus to be with him in his boat, where he watches out for you, even though to human eyes it might appear that he has fallen asleep: "Why are you terrified, O you of little faith?" (Mt 8:26). Unconditional and fearless faith in the close presence of the Lord must be the compass that guides your working and family life toward God, from whom all light and happiness flows.

The world in which we live has need — as do you — of this faith, of this lighthouse. To forget God would mean sinking into the solitude of the shadows, being left with no course and no steering. For that reason, dear brothers, I strongly encourage you to cultivate the faith you have been given.

MEETING WITH SEAFARERS, SANTIAGO DE COMPOSTELA, SPAIN
November 9, 1982

You who are present today, tell those who have lost heart, tell them especially through the testimony of your own life: courage! Above all those young people who grow up in surroundings of subculture, superstition, and violence, at the mercy of the urban underclass, easy prey to corruption, violence, and drugs—for these young people, be available for service, solidarity, and a concrete, timely, effective commitment. Together with them, construct a new future and a new society, in which there is justice and work for all; unemployment is death to young people. A new future and a new society, in which drugs are no more; drugs are a hatchet blow to the roots of being. A new future and a new society, in which there is no more violence or war. Peace is possible; peace is not a dream, not a utopia. A new future and a new society, in which the ramifications of the Mafioso mindset of some, the perpetrators of aberrant manifestations of criminality, are isolated and destroyed.

MEETING WITH YOUTH, PALERMO, ITALY
November 21, 1982

The task of every Christian worker, and of every workers' association, is to be the bearer, the herald, and the witness of what I have chosen to call "the Gospel of work" (John Paul II, *Laborem Exercens*, 6–7, 25–26). By the light of this Gospel, the machine shop operator or the field hand, the office clerk or the trained professional, or anyone at all who pursues an occupation, discovers that "the basis for determining the value of human work is not primarily the kind of work being done but the fact that the one who is doing it is a person" (Ibid, 6). It is on this principle that the true meaning and worth of the work and the dignity of the worker are based.

The work of a man — whatever work, physical or intellectual — is an act of a human person; all work has its human value and every worker has the dignity of a human person.

SPEECH TO THE CHRISTIAN WORKERS' MOVEMENT
December 19, 1982

Beloved brothers and children,

Infirmity and pain have taken possession of your fragile bodies, preventing you from leading a life normal for your age, happily surrounded by your parents and friends. That is why your friend the Pope, who so often thinks of you and prays for you, has chosen to come here to visit you. In order that you might receive every day the affection and care that you need, through your parents and relatives, the doctors and all the other staff, whom I also greet and encourage to continue in their service to you with an authentic spirit of dedication to those who suffer. I ask that in their work they remember the words of Jesus: "Whatever you did for one of these least brothers of mine, you did for me" (Mt 25:40).

GREETING TO SICK CHILDREN, SAN JOSÉ, COSTA RICA
March 3, 1983

At this point we can understand the deeper meaning of study and work at the same time: the quest for holiness. The task that lies ahead of you as you pursue a Christian testimony in university work can therefore be expressed in a word with great content: holiness. Holiness in study and through study. The world of work has need of your holy lives. And this holy life is made up of doctrine and prayer, intimacy with Christ and work: it is made up of Love. The reason for this? I take it from words that are certainly well known to you: "Your human vocation is a part, and an important part, of your divine vocation. That is the reason you must strive for holiness, contributing at the same time to the holiness of others, your fellow men, in sanctifying your work and your environment: the profession or job that fills your day, which gives a particular character to your human personality, your lifestyle" (Josemaría Escrivá, *Pasa Jesús* [Jesus is passing by], § 46).

I have noticed that you, traveling through the expanses of the skies, are particularly positioned to read the fascinating book of nature, which lies open to your eyes when you fly over various territories, and which illustrates and magnifies the greatness of the Almighty, as the psalmist sings in inspired tones: "The heavens declare the glory of God; the sky proclaims its builder's craft" (Ps 19).

Take inspiration from these poetic visions to cultivate in your hearts the sentiments of the great, the noble, and the beautiful, to dispose your minds to an ever more generous practice, and to educate your souls to peace, harmony, and brotherhood, in the clear awareness that none of what you have done here below, with the support of faith, Christian love, and human solidarity, will be wasted as something ephemeral, but will endure and will bear fruit in the eternal life.

SPEECH TO THE 31ST WING OF THE ITALIAN AIR FORCE
April 2, 1983

Your specialization unquestionably imposes upon you certain rules and indispensable limitations in your investigations, but beyond these epistemological boundaries, allow the inclinations of your spirit to carry you toward the universal and the absolute. More than ever, our world has need of intelligent minds capable of grasping broad concepts and helping knowledge to progress toward humane understanding and wisdom. In short, your science must expand into wisdom, that is to say, it must become the development of man, of the whole man. Open entirely your minds and your hearts to the imperatives of the world of today, which aspires to a justice and a dignity founded upon truth. And may you yourselves be open to the search for all that is true, in the persuasion that the realities of the soul form part of reality and Truth as a whole.

SPEECH TO A GROUP OF SCIENTISTS AND RESEARCHERS
May 9, 1983

Do not be afraid of Christ! I repeat this today to you and to all young people! He does not take away your identity; he does not dishonor, debase, or affront your reason; he does not oppress your freedom! He is the Son of God, who was incarnated, who died, and who rose again for us and for our salvation, that is to say, for our authentic and total liberation! He, God, truly chose to become one of us, our Savior, our Redeemer, our Friend, our Brother; he took part in our problems and our everyday tragedies; he shared our weakness, our fragility, our precariousness, all the way up to the anguishing experience of betrayal by those close to him and the pain of death. As the incarnation of the infinite mercy of God, Christ extended his message of truth and hope to humanity, he performed miracles, he obtained the forgiveness of sins, but above all he offered himself to his Father in an act of immense love, as victim in expiation of our sins!

SPEECH TO YOUTH, MONZA, ITALY
May 21, 1983

It is impossible to remain indifferent in the presence of Christ! We are not merely in the presence of a Teacher, however illustrious, of ideologies with an ethical foundation; or in the presence of a man with a particular religious experience; or of a great prophet; or a privileged man, in whom a special moral presence of God manifested itself. Personalities of that kind may be of interest for a certain period in our historic, literary, philosophical, or religious studies. Christ, by his singular human and divine reality, and by the unique mission he received from his Father, takes in and encompasses all of our human experience, because he is the Center of History, the Redeemer of Humanity!

SPEECH TO YOUTH, MONZA, ITALY
May 21, 1983

What a stupendous mystery! In order to reach Christ, it is not necessary to reach back in time to the days of his earthly life, nor must we travel in space and cross the borders of Palestine. It is enough to enter a church, to draw near to a tabernacle: we find him there; we can speak to him; we can listen to his inspirations; we can adore him. My first words, in this meeting of ours, are meant as an invitation to join with all the other faithful who kneel before the Eucharist and worship it.

MEETING WITH WORKERS, SESTO SAN GIOVANNI, ITALY
May 21, 1983

Mary is the highest testament to what the Spirit of God can create in man, when it renews him in the intimacy of his soul and constitutes him as living rock in a new world. Preceded by the Grace of the Redeemer, she responded with faithful obedience to all of God's requests, and every impulse of the Holy Spirit: as humble handmaiden, she bestowed herself virginally upon the Lord; as a caring sister, she was attentive to the needs of others; as a mother, she consecrated herself entirely to the person and the mission of her son the Redeemer, becoming a perfect disciple to him and associating herself generously with him in the one and only sacrifice that erases sin and reconciles us with our Father. The Holy Spirit illuminated for her the dark path of faith every step of the way, enlightened every word and every act of her son, supported her in the grief and pain of Calvary and the supreme sacrifice. Then, after the Cross, he configured her to him in glory.

ANGELUS, MILAN, ITALY
May 22, 1983

May your profession, which demands so much training and is so beloved by the crowds, encourage you and your colleagues to be, not only champions in sport, but also outstanding champions in life, capable of distinguishing yourselves in the pursuit of the true values that make a man great as a human person, that is, which make him more of a man.

Indeed, you also have social responsibility: fans appreciate the athletic talent of a player, which arouses their enthusiasm; but their thoughts also go, sometimes perhaps subconsciously, to the man, to the person, to his moral merits and his values; and so, with your honesty, your sincerity, and your sense of duty you can contribute to the moral formation of society and especially of young people.

The sincere wish that I extend to you is that your lives, aside from expressing themselves in athletic victories, aim also and especially toward the higher ideal of a full human and Christian achievement.

SPEECH TO THE MANAGERS AND PLAYERS OF A. S. ROMA
June 10, 1983

You are moving toward other people. Many of them are still unknown to you. One may perhaps become the companion of your life, decisive for you as well as for the children of whom you will be parents. How will you meet? How will you learn the love that overcomes even disappointments? How will you learn the true self-realization that not only knows the word "me" but also "you" and "us"? Jesus said, "Take my yoke upon you, and learn from me!" (Mt 11:29).

You are also moving toward work, and I hope with all my heart that you all, in fact, find work. For many, it will not be the work that they dreamed of, but instead quite simply a job, where you will nonetheless be expected to devote all your effort and commitment. Work in a loyal manner, be good colleagues. And when the time comes, be willing to take on special responsibilities. Don't be afraid to declare yourselves as Christians in your workplace. This creed will bring you profound joy, even if sometimes you will not be understood or may even be mocked.

MEETING WITH YOUTH, VIENNA, AUSTRIA
September 10, 1983

You want a society with greater sincerity, justice, and mercy. You want a society with a greater sense of responsibility toward your fellow man and the environment, greater tolerance, and above all a more peaceful world. Begin by being more sincere and just, more merciful and committed to peace, the peace that we can expect from others only if we live that peace ourselves.

MEETING WITH YOUTH, VIENNA, AUSTRIA
September 10, 1983

I turn my gaze especially toward you, bent down with the weight of years, suffering as you do with the limitations and aches and pains of old age. You too require our help, and yet it is you who give gifts to us. It is on the foundation of your work, your accomplishments, everything that you have, as it were, invested for us, that we continue to build. We need your experience and your judgment. We need your experience of faith and your example. Do not shut yourselves away. You must not remain outside the doors of our homes and the gates of our world. You are part of us! A society that turns its back on the elderly would not only deny its own origin, but would deny itself its very future.

MEETING WITH THE ELDERLY, VIENNA, AUSTRIA
September 11, 1983

Neither the old nor the sick should be marginalized. Their presence is important. We all have a debt of gratitude to them. At this time, I would like to thank all of you who, at various moments of humanity's need, have offered up your suffering and your prayers. Of course, the healthy must also pray, but your prayers have a special weight. You can call down rivers of blessings from heaven and you can bestow them upon your friends, your homeland, and all the men and women who are in need of God's help.

MEETING WITH THE ELDERLY, VIENNA, AUSTRIA
September 11, 1983

Man and his world—our Earth that appeared during the first journey into space as a star colored green and sky blue—must be protected and helped to progress. That means that life should be dealt with cautiously, including animal life and all of nature, animate and inanimate. The Earth, within the perspective of faith, is not a reservoir to be exploited without restraint. Rather, it is a part of the mystery of Creation. It is there for us not only to use, but to accord awe and reverence.

MEETING WITH ACADEMICS AND ARTISTS, VIENNA, AUSTRIA
September 12, 1983

Handmaid of man: this is a fine definition of art, a good mission for art. But art serves that mission only if it links its liberty to humanity. In turn, humanity makes itself manifest with all its hopes, but also with all its dangers, only when it is viewed in the realm of the infinite, in the realm of God, who is absolutely at the foundation of all of man's desires and aspirations, and who alone can satisfy them.

Both the individual and the community need art to interpret the world and life, to illuminate the large picture of an era, to comprehend the depths and heights of existence. They need art to establish contact with that which transcends the sphere of the purely useful and therefore elevates man. They need literature and poetry: their words, sometimes gentle and delicate, and at others prophetically angry, which often ripen in loneliness and suffering. According to a profound thought of Beethoven, the artist is in a certain sense summoned to a priestly service.

MEETING WITH ACADEMICS AND ARTISTS, VIENNA, AUSTRIA
September 12, 1983

I have been able to talk personally with each one of you. Perhaps you have told me things you prepared in advance, as if you were following an outline. Others have chosen to make a small confession. I have told you what I had in my heart. I assure you that I am willing to do anything for you, to be near you always. I will do for you whatever I am able.

The presence of Mary, Mother of Christ, is close to us. I entrust each one of you to this Mother. Because she is the source of our consolation and therefore of our hopes. Because the Mother of Christ, and our Mother, can give you the love of God as a gift. I want to entrust you to this Mother and I want this Mother to be among you as a sweet, utterly sweet presence.

Today I have been able to meet with my attempted assassin and repeat my forgiveness of him, as I did immediately, as soon as I was able. We meet as men and brothers, and all the experiences of our lives lead to this brotherhood.

MEETING WITH INMATES OF REBIBBIA PRISON, ROME, ITALY
December 27, 1983

In connection with Christ the Savior and his sacrifice, let us contemplate first of all the Virgin Mary. It was to her that Simeon, illuminated by the Holy Spirit, addressed mysterious, prophetic words: "and you yourself a sword will pierce" (Lk 2:35). It is an annunciation that will culminate for Mary in the Passion and Death of her Son. Near him, as he is pierced by the spear on Mount Calvary, is his Mother, whose soul is pierced by a sword. And the Word of God is compared to a sword. Because of the Word that creates and destroys, that gives death and life; because of the Word that Mary is not able to understand immediately, but which she accepts and reflects upon and engages in her heart; because of Christ who is the Word of the Father, contradicted by men, her heart is pierced by pain like a sword. The Word, accepted and experienced in total obedience to the Father, makes the Virgin the generous collaborator of Christ the Savior. Her sacrifice joined with that of Christ brings light and salvation to the people.

ANGELUS
January 15, 1984

You have been close to the evil of hatred and its worst expression, which is war. At the same time you have shared the dream of countless ordinary and upright people for peace and reconciliation, and for the harmony and brotherhood that transcend all diversity and differences.

Your own presence was intended to help create conditions to favor peace.

Here you are witnesses, together with fellow pilgrims from all over the world, to the constructive power inherent in the unity of the one human family: the power to live together, to work together, and together to look upward to the God and Father of us all. Dear friends, may the fatherhood of God enable you to understand ever better the brotherhood of man and the harmony and love that must characterize all human relationships. And may God's love touch the hearts of all of you today.

SPEECH TO U.S. NAVY MEMBERS OF THE LEBANON PEACEKEEPING FORCE, ROME, ITALY
January 25, 1984

Allow me to address you thus: Friends! Not only because of the relationship that this meeting confirms: a relationship of esteem, reciprocal trust; and therefore, of friendship. But you are also friends because—let me assure you immediately, from my heart, of the high consideration in which the Church and the Apostolic See hold your profession—one might say that you are our fellow travelers. In fact, you are professional communicators. And evangelizing, which is the Church's primary task, evangelizing, as an annunciation of the kingdom, isn't it too, first and foremost, communication?

SPEECH TO JOURNALISTS
January 27, 1984

Down through the centuries and generations it has been seen that in suffering there is concealed a particular power that draws a person interiorly close to Christ, a special grace. To this grace many saints, such as Saint Francis of Assisi, Saint Ignatius of Loyola, and others, owe their profound conversion. A result of such a conversion is not only that the individual discovers the salvific meaning of suffering but above all that he becomes a completely new person. He discovers a new dimension, as it were, of his entire life and vocation. This discovery is a particular confirmation of the spiritual greatness, which in man surpasses the body in a way that is completely beyond compare. When this body is gravely ill, totally incapacitated, and the person is almost incapable of living and acting, all the more do interior maturity and spiritual greatness become evident, constituting a touching lesson to those who are healthy and normal.

APOSTOLIC LETTER SALVIFICI DOLORIS, § 26
February 11, 1984

We were not the ones to lay the foundations. It was He who created us. We must receive ourselves from his hand. Many men of our time are no longer willing to accept this fact: that we are as we are, that is, with certain characteristics, with a certain prior history, at a certain stage of the world, in a certain social and cultural condition. To say yes to myself; to say yes to the fact that God causes me to live here and now, thus and not otherwise; to say yes to my own limitations, but also to say yes to you, to my neighbor, to the fact that he was created by God as he is: all of this inevitably forms part of our yes to God.

SPEECH TO FAMILIES
March 25, 1984

The place where we meet tonight speaks to us in a particular way with the language of the Cross of Christ, because it takes us back in our thoughts to the centuries in which the Christians were persecuted.

They left us a testimony of heroic sacrifice, and in them "death and life met in a tremendous duel" (Easter liturgy). Even though in the eyes of men death seems to have prevailed, according to the divine economy of redemption, they have received possession of the fullness of life.

And so they live in God himself, joined in the mystery of communion of the saints, in which—in a eternal bond with Christ crucified and risen—they are joined, at the same time, with the earthly Church in the Jubilee of Redemption.

We therefore wish to sense in a particularly profound manner their presence in this place. We wish to enter into the inheritance of their merits, which are all the fruit of the Cross of Christ. With such faith, we meditate upon their martyrdom, daring to say, in the words of the apostle, that with their sufferings they have completed what was lacking in the sufferings of Christ.

SPEECH AT THE END OF THE WAY OF THE CROSS AT THE COLOSSEUM, ROME, ITALY
April 20, 1984

Jesus is important for you because he is the Son of God who became man. He teaches you the deepest meaning of life: who you are and what life is all about. In knowing Jesus, in studying his teaching in the Gospels, you will also get to understand yourselves more fully.

And you are important for Jesus because he loves you and died for you, so that you might live the fullness of life, both here on Earth and later on in heaven. Yes, you are very important for Jesus. And you are very important for me and for the whole Church.

You have a special mission to perform in life; there is a particular task marked out for each and every one of you. And to succeed in life you must remain united to Jesus; you must listen to him when he tells you, "Remain in my love" (Jn 15:9).

SPEECH TO YOUTH, PORT MORESBY, PAPUA NEW GUINEA
May 8, 1984

Listen to these words that come from my heart: I want you to know of my love. We are truly brothers and sisters, members of the same human family, sons and daughters of the same loving Father. I wish to share with you your sufferings, your hardships, your pain, so that you may know that someone cares for you, sympathizes with your plight, and works to help you find relief, comfort, and a reason for hope.

Have faith in yourselves. Never forget your identity as free people who have a rightful place in this world. Never lose your personality as a people! Remain firmly rooted in your respective cultures, from which the world can learn much and come to appreciate you in your uniqueness.

Have hope in the future. Our world is in full development. It needs you and your contributions. Take every opportunity offered to you to study a language and perfect a skill, in order to be able to adapt socially to the country that will open its doors to you and be enriched by your presence.

SPEECH TO REFUGEES IN PHANAT NIKHOM CAMP, THAILAND
May 11, 1984

First of all, a word of hope. Certainly, it might seem at first glance a word that is out of place here. This setting and your suffering seem to speak an entirely different language to you. And yet I feel the audacity to tell you that you must, that you can hope. I am speaking of Christian hope, the hope that springs from the certainty that God loves us, his creatures, that he is the Father of Mercy, that he sent us his son Jesus that we might all be saved.

With hope, behold also the gift of faith. Faith in God, first and foremost; and through him, faith in yourselves and in other men. How I would like to persuade you that the Lord is the first to believe and have faith in you! With him, I too have faith in your possibilities for good, which are numerous and perhaps far greater than you yourselves imagine; I am sure that you will succeed in developing all the good potential and attitudes that you harbor in your hearts. Whatever your past and however difficult the future may promise to be, know that your Lord will not abandon you, but will stand at your side and support you.

SPEECH TO PRISON INMATES, VITERBO, ITALY
May 27, 1984

Yes, beloved invalids who have gathered here under the weight of the Cross, and all you faithful who accompany them, bringing your hearts oppressed by the weight of affliction: know that Holy Mary, Mother of the Redeemer and our Mother, wishes to conduct you to a meeting with Christ the Liberator. Guided by her maternal hand, day after day, you are called to an endless succession of meetings with Christ who frees us from evil. As we read in the Letter to the Hebrews (12:12–13): "So strengthen your drooping hands and your weak knees. Make straight paths for your feet, that what is lame may not be dislocated but healed."

Beloved invalids, ask Holy Mary Liberator for the grace to understand, and to help those who are close to you to understand, that any liberation is ephemeral and illusory unless it frees us from sin, the root of evil and death.

SPEECH TO THE SICK, VITERBO, ITALY
May 27, 1984

The continuous course of history requires an endless stream of new apostles, to announce the Gospel and to live in the heart of temporal life, like yeast in dough. These new apostles will be fervent disciples of Jesus Christ, completely integrated into their own time and the different milieus in which they live. They will be, at the same time, Christians deeply engaged in the apostolic movement that is best suited to their social and professional status and unfailingly focused on living in a complementary situation with other associations. The exercise of the apostolate is all the more credible and effective the more the movements accept their diversity and contribute to the same objective of evangelization in a fraternal collaboration: in that case, they represent a treasure for the unity of the Church in a state of mission.

SPEECH TO LAITY INVOLVED IN THE APOSTOLATE, EINSIEDELN, SWITZERLAND
June 15, 1984

"We want to be able to shout, with conviction and sincerity, that young people together with Christ are a force that, starting from the Gospels and propelled by the Spirit, transform man, society, and the Church." That is your answer, and I am fully in accord with it, young friends, you who represent so many thousands of boys and girls from every part of the country, many of whom were unable to come here with us. Your festive, happy presence, your thirst for truth and noble and elevated ideals encourage me to continue to believe in and place hope in young people. As does the Church, which at the conclusion of the Second Vatican Council proclaimed, thinking of you: "The Church looks to you with faith and love" (Message to Young People, § 6, December 8, 1965).

MEETING WITH YOUTH, CARACAS, VENEZUELA
January 28, 1985

I now wish to speak urgently to the men who have placed their faith in armed struggle, those who have been deceived by false ideologies, to the point of believing that terror and violence, by exacerbating the already lamentable social tensions and forcing a supreme clash, can lead to a better world.

To them, I wish to say: Evil is never the path to good! You cannot destroy the lives of your brothers; you cannot continue to sow panic among mothers, wives, and daughters. You cannot continue to threaten the elderly. Not only are you deviating from the path that the God of love has shown us with his life, but you are hindering the development of your people.

The merciless logic of violence leads nowhere! You cannot achieve any good ends by contributing to its increase. If your objective is to create a more just and fraternal Peru, seek the paths of dialogue and not those of violence.

APPEAL TO THE MEN OF THE ARMED STRUGGLE (SHINING PATH), AYACUCHO, PERU
February 3, 1985

Yes, "everyone is looking for you" (Mk 1:37), O Jesus Christ! Many seek you directly, calling you by name, with faith, hope, and charity. There are some who search for you indirectly: through others. And there are others who search for you without knowing it. . . . And there are even those who search even though they deny the search.

Nonetheless, everyone is searching for you, they are searching for you first and foremost because you search for them first; because you became a man, in the Virgin Mother's womb, for everyone; because you redeemed everyone at the cost of your Cross. Thus you opened, in the intricate and impracticable paths of the human heart and the fate of man, the way. You who are the way, the truth, and the life, we address you in this prayer through the heart of your Mother, the Virgin, Mary the most holy.

ANGELUS
February 10, 1985

Today man is riven with an existential disquiet that manifests, in different forms and tones, his need for salvation, liberation, and peace. Through the significant encounters of his life, he learns to appreciate the value of the constituent dimensions of his own being, first and foremost the dimensions of religion, the family, and the people to whom he belongs. Still, sooner or later, he realizes to a dramatic degree that he does not yet possess the ultimate significance of those encounters, capable of making them definitively good, true, and beautiful. And he then feels an inherent inability to appease his need for the infinite.

He is thus placed before a tremendous either/or: to demand that Another appear on the horizon of his existence to reveal and render possible its complete fulfillment, or to withdraw into himself, in existential solitude in which the very positivity of being is denied. The shouted demand, or the blasphemy: that is all that remains to him!

SPEECH TO THE CONGRESS "BRINGING CHRIST TO MAN"
February 22, 1985

The conversion of the heart cannot fail to include penitence. In a certain sense, that is its principal element; in fact, its essential element. Penitence means a profound change of heart under the influence of the word of God and in the prospect of the kingdom; it is a commitment to restore the equilibrium and harmony shattered by sin and therefore to change direction, even at the cost of sacrifice. The resolutions of conversion and repentance, in order to be authentic and enduring, must be translated into concrete penitential acts. Between what one is deep in one's inner heart and the actions that constitute the fabric of one's existence, there cannot be anything less than a clear and faithful consistency. Repentance, therefore, is the conversion that passes from one's heart to one's works and, thus, to the entire life of a Christian.

ANGELUS
March 3, 1985

"Jesus, looking at him, loved him" (Mk 10:21). May you experience a look like that! May you experience the truth that he, Christ, looks upon you with love!

He looks with love upon every human being. The Gospel confirms this at every step. One can also say that this "loving look" of Christ contains, as it were, a summary and synthesis of the entire Good News. If we would seek the beginning of this look, we must turn back to the book of Genesis, to that instant when, after the creation of man "male and female," God "looked . . . and he found it very good" (Gn 1:31). That very first look of the Creator is reflected in the look of Christ that accompanies his conversation with the young man in the Gospel.

APOSTOLIC LETTER DILECTI AMICI (TO YOUTH), § 7
March 31, 1985

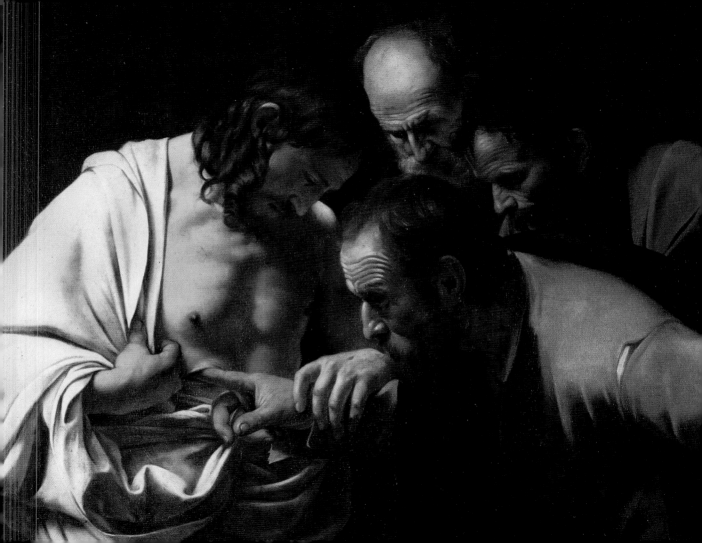

The law of God written in people's hearts and proclaimed by the Church . . . speaks a language that everyone can understand, like the parable of the Good Samaritan. It provides an answer for man's desire for a meaning to life, a life that does not end with death. It expresses what people may expect from one another.

Jesus Christ preached a kingdom of truth, love, and peace — three indivisible elements. People must want these elements to come into their lives and into their relations with others. Peace only comes when human beings strive for truth and love in their dealing with one another, when they discover who they really are and recognize one another's purpose.

SPEECH TO THE INTERNATIONAL COURT OF JUSTICE, THE HAGUE, NETHERLANDS
May 13, 1985

The heart of Jesus was formed by the Holy Spirit in the womb of the Virgin Mother. God, who gives the life that is conceded to man, began his work of the economy of salvation by becoming a man. It was precisely in the virginal conception and the birth from Mary that his human heart had its beginning, formed by the Holy Spirit in the womb of the Virgin Mother. We wish to venerate this heart during the month of June. This very day, we wish to make this heart a singular repository for the trust of our own poor human hearts, of the hearts that have been tested in various ways, in different manners oppressed. And also of the hearts that are trusting in the power of God himself and in the saving power of the Most Holy Trinity. Mary, Virgin Mother, you who know better than we can the divine heart of your Son, join with us this day in our adoration of the Most Holy Trinity, together with a humble prayer for the Church and for the world!

ANGELUS
June 2, 1985

The pursuit of sports always reminds us of the ideals of human and Christian virtues, which not only contribute to physical and mental training, but promote and encourage strength and moral and spiritual greatness. Sports are a school for loyalty, courage, tolerance, will power, solidarity, and team spirit. All of these natural virtues are, frequently, the foundation upon which other supernatural virtues are consolidated.

In your lives as professional cyclists and in your family and social responsibilities, do not forget to put into practice that series of small and great acts of self-control, simplicity, honesty, and respect for others that are learned in the arena of sports. Shun all that is disloyalty, deceit, and cheating because that degrades your profession and diminishes you in the eyes of God.

SPEECH TO THE SPANISH CYCLING TEAM ZOR
June 10, 1985

Everyone who has been baptized must be an apostle. That is, someone sent to transmit everywhere the light of the Gospel, to bring to every walk of life the force of Christian ferment.

My young friends! The world of other young people your age, the fields of culture and art, the sector of civic and political life, like every field of human endeavor and pursuit, cannot be alien to your commitment to the apostolate. I speak of the individual apostolate and the collective apostolate. Remember this always: on your commitment depends much of the progress of civilization and the culture of love, so immensely needed in our time.

SPEECH TO YOUTH, TERAMO, ITALY
June 30, 1985

Spread joy in the surroundings in which you live or are active: in the family, in the school, in the places of work and of play; above all spread joy to those who are alone, old, sick, or marginalized from society; to those who are absorbed in the daily rat race; to those who vainly seek joy where it is least to be found: in the murderous surrogates of drugs and alcohol; or in the fatal and empty recourse to consumerism and lack of commitment; and especially to those who have succumbed to the influence of the deplorable movements impelled in any way toward violence or lack of respect for others. To all these brothers and sisters who, in one way or another, consciously or unconsciously, are awaiting from you a word, a smile, and your friendship, do not fail to offer your presence, do not refuse to show your joy, and the reasons for your hope.

SPEECH TO YOUTH, TERAMO, ITALY
June 30, 1985

It was in the womb of Mary that the man and the heart were both conceived. This heart is – just like any human heart – a center, a sanctuary in which the spiritual life pulsates with a special rhythm. The heart, irreplaceable resonance of everything that the spirit of man experiences. Every human heart is summoned to beat with the rhythm of justice and charity. This is the measure of man's true dignity. The heart of Jesus beats with the rhythm of justice and love to the same divine measure! This, in fact, is the heart of the man-God. In it, all justice of God toward man must be achieved until the end and also, to a certain degree, the justice of man toward God. In the human heart of the Son of God, the justice of God himself is offered to humanity. This justice is at the same time the gift of love. It is through the heart of Jesus that love entered the history of humanity as enduring love: "For God so loved the world that he gave his only Son" (Jn 3:16).

ANGELUS
July 14, 1985

Mary says, "May it be done to me according to your word" (Lk 1:38). And from that moment her heart prepares to receive the man-God: "*Heart of Jesus, worthy of all praise!*" We join with the Mother of God to adore this heart of man that, through the mystery of the hypostatic union (union of natures), is at the same time the heart of God. We render unto God the adoration due to the heart of Christ Jesus, from the very moment of his conception in the womb of the Virgin. Together with Mary we render unto him the same adoration at the moment of birth: when he comes into the world in the extreme poverty of Bethlehem. We render unto him, together with Mary, the same adoration for all the days and years of his life hidden away in Nazareth, for all the days and years in which he performed his messianic service in Israel. And when the time comes for the Passion, the spoliation, the humiliation, and the opprobrium of the Cross, we join even more ardently with the heart of the Mother to shout: "*Heart of Jesus, worthy of all praise!*"

Salꝟe Mater pietatis et totius Trinitatis nobile Triclinium

Christians and Muslims, we have many things in common, as believers and as human beings. We live in the same world, marked by many signs of hope, but also by multiple signs of anguish. For us, Abraham is a very model of faith in God, of submission to his will and of confidence in his goodness. We believe in the same God, the one God, the living God, the God who created the world and brings his creatures to their perfection.

It is therefore toward this God that my thought goes and that my heart rises: it is of God himself that, above all, I wish to speak with you; of him, because it is in him that we believe, you Muslims and we Catholics. I wish also to speak with you about human values, which have their basis in God, these values which concern the blossoming of our person, as also that of our families and our societies, as well as that of the international community. The mystery of God, is it not the highest reality from which depends the very meaning that man gives to his life?

SPEECH TO YOUNG MUSLIMS, CASABLANCA, MOROCCO
August 19, 1985

Human knowledge is like the water of our springs: those who drink from them become thirsty once again. The wisdom and knowledge of Jesus, on the other hand, open the eyes of the mind, move the heart in the depth of the being, and engender in man transcendent love; they free him from the shadows of error, from the stains of sin, from the danger of death, and lead to the fullness of the communion of those divine goods that transcend the comprehension of the human mind. With the wisdom and knowledge of Jesus, we are rooted and grounded in love (Eph 3:17). A new, inner man is created, who places God in the center of his life and himself at the service of his brothers.

ANGELUS
September 1, 1985

In this aspiration to something more, which is implacable in the soul of a young person, and therefore beneficent and blessed, I wish to confirm you. It is Peter, a "rock" by divine calling, as we hear also in the song composed for this occasion, who exhorts you not to settle into mediocrity, not to become addicted to worldly desires, not to live your lives only by halves, with your aspirations reduced or, worse, atrophied. The Pope has come to invite you to take this path, to the continually new things to be sought inside yourself, with your own life. Don't "let life happen"; take your life into your own hands and make the decision to turn it into an authentic and personal masterpiece!

MEETING WITH YOUTH, GENOA, ITALY
September 22, 1985

We must be the defenders of man, of every man, of all men. We must restore them to themselves, wherever their sacred dignity is put in danger, wherever their fundamental liberties have been unjustly undermined or even annihilated, wherever their innate need of openness to the Absolute is treated as an enslaving illusion and methodically combated.

92

SPEECH TO FORMER DEPORTEES OF THE SECOND WORLD WAR
September 26, 1985

Through work, man can fulfill himself as a Christian and, in a certain sense, be more Christian. This becomes possible when man, giving the meaning to work that it has in the eyes of God, allows himself to be guided by faith, hope, and charity. He then draws closer to God, enters the enterprise of salvation, and his work becomes an exercise of faith and a stimulus to elevation and prayer.

MEETING WITH THE MINERS OF MONTEPONI, CAGLIARI, ITALY
October 18, 1985

"The joys and the hopes, the griefs and the anxieties of the men of this age, especially those who are poor or in any way afflicted, these are the joys and hopes, the griefs and anxieties of the followers of Christ. Indeed, nothing genuinely human fails to raise an echo in their hearts" (Paul VI, *Gaudium et spes*, § 1). . . . In our pursuit of the great objectives of human elevation, no interest drives us, no ambition seduces us, that is not in the service of the good of man himself, understood in the truth of his being and his temporal and eternal destiny. Nor does it eclipse in any way the transcendence of our religious conceptions, which is indeed a corroborating and stimulating, as well as specific, factor in the ecclesial solidarity with the cause of man.

ANGELUS
November 10, 1985

From this place, which belongs in a sense to the history of the entire human family, I wish, however, to reaffirm the conviction that with the help of God the construction of a better world, in peace and justice, lies within the reach of human beings.

But the leaders of peoples, and all men and women of good will, must believe and act of the belief that the solution lies within the human heart: "from a new heart, peace is born." . . . Mahatma Gandhi reveals to us his own heart as he repeats today to those who listen: "The law of love governs the world. . . . Truth triumphs over untruth. Love conquers hate."

SPEECH AT THE GANDHI MONUMENT, RAJ GHAT, DELHI, INDIA
February 1, 1986

"The Angel of the Lord declared unto Mary, and she conceived of the Holy Spirit."

Mary conceived the eternal Son of God.

"And the Word was made flesh and dwelt among us."

It is this great mystery that we ponder each day in the Angelus: God became man in the womb of Mary.

Through this great mystery, all human life was changed. Humanity received a new dignity. God became one with us in all things but sin, so that we might become one with God. The moment Mary said yes—"Be it done unto me according to your word"—God came down to Earth, and the life of every man and woman was lifted up. We human beings were brought close to God by God drawing near to us. But not only that—we were also brought closer to one another.

The Eternal Word, the Son of God, was made man and became our brother in the flesh. As a result, we are closely bound together as brothers and sisters in the Lord.

ANGELUS
February 2, 1986

In Nirmal Hriday, the mystery of human suffering meets the mystery of faith and love. And in this meeting, the deepest questions of human existence make themselves heard. The pain-filled body and spirit cries out: "Why? What is the purpose of suffering? Why must I die?" And the answer that comes, often in unspoken ways of kindness and compassion, is filled with honesty and faith: "I cannot fully answer all your questions; I cannot take away all your pain. But of this I am sure: God loves you with an everlasting love. You are precious in his sight. In him I love you too. For in God we are truly brothers and sisters."

The loving care which is shown here bears witness to the truth that the worth of a human being is not measured by usefulness or talents, by health or sickness, by age or creed or race. Our human dignity comes from God our Creator in whose image we are all made. No amount of privation or suffering can ever remove this dignity, for we are always precious in the eyes of God.

SPEECH AT MOTHER TERESA'S HOSPICE NIRMAL HRIDAY, KOLKATA, INDIA
February 3, 1986

Mary of Nazareth is indeed worthy of our veneration and filial love. "She cooperated by her obedience, faith, hope, and ardent charity in the Savior's work" (Paul VI, *Lumen Gentium*, 61). She changed all of human history by her "Fiat," by her free consent to the will of God. By this act of faith and love, she allowed herself to be transformed by God. Submitting herself totally to God, she agreed to be the Mother of the Redeemer of the world: the eternal Word became flesh, God became man. From the moment of the Annunciation, she dedicated herself to her Son, to his person and to his work, to the mystery of the redemption that he accomplished. From that day forward and for all time, she assists her Son in his mission of salvation. In every age, Mary is close to the Church, the Body of Christ. And thus, she is rightly called "Mother of the Church."

ANGELUS, BASILICA OF OUR LADY OF THE MOUNT, MUMBAI, INDIA
February 9, 1986

Man presents himself to the presence of God in all his inner truth. This is the truth of the conscience. Reflected in it is the moral law that is known to man: in fact, it is not only confirmed by revelation, but it is also written in the hearts of one and all. This law culminates in the commandment of love. By the light of this law—and to an even greater degree, in the light of the love revealed in the Cross of Christ—man sees his own life and his own behavior, his own thoughts, words, and works. He sees in the truth. And through this truth he encounters God. He cannot meet with him except in the truth. It is in this that the irreplaceable greatness of the conscience consists. Lent summons and exhorts our consciences with particular vigor.

ANGELUS
February 16, 1986

"For I know my offense; my sin is always before me" (Ps 51:5).

So many people have been aided by this wonderful text about the inner truth of the conscience, to penetrate their deeper selves. They have been helped to call evil by its true name, evil that is in man and whose cause is man.

An examination of one's conscience is always a rereading of the deepest truth about oneself, a truth that can never be erased. The greatness of man lies in this truth. The dignity of a human being demands that man be able to call it by its name, and not falsify it.

And when man—together with the psalmist—confesses, "My sin is always before me," he recognizes, at the same time, that the very power of an inner truth commands him to proceed, and to say, "Against you . . . have I sinned."

ANGELUS
February 23, 1986

Sin is against God. . . . At the same time it is a drama that takes place between God and man. God is not indifferent to sin.

But even if my sin is against God, God is not against me! In the moment of the inner tension of the human conscience, God does not pronounce his sentence. He does not condemn. God waits for me to turn to him, as to loving Justice, as to the Father, as is taught in the parable of the prodigal son. That I might reveal my sin to him. And that I might entrust myself to him. In this way, from the examination of conscience we pass on to what constitutes the very substance of conversion and reconciliation with God.

ANGELUS
February 23, 1986

It is certainly true that the genius of an artist can create eminent works in that field, whatever the state of his religious faith; but if to his natural talent are consciously added the fully embraced theological virtues of faith, hope, and charity, these become powerful stimuli to his work as he attempts to illustrate with the magisterium of art the mysteries of Christianity.

We thus understand the wonderful flourishing of cathedrals in the Middle Ages. We cannot explain this without faith, alongside the genius of their creators, the works of Giotto, Fra Angelico, Michelangelo, and the poetry of Dante and the prose of Manzoni, the musical compositions of Pierluigi da Palestrina, to name only a few.

Artists should be counted among the greatest benefactors of mankind, among the strongest forces on behalf of humanity's salvation, because they encourage the qualifying, essential sense of man, which is his spirituality.

SPEECH TO THE CATHOLIC UNION OF ITALIAN ARTISTS
March 1, 1986

Dear young people, look to Jesus, look at his hidden life in Nazareth. Jesus, who was young just like you, adopted your age as well, and therefore he included it in his great plan of redemption and salvation. Everything in our human condition that was assumed into the Divine Word through his Incarnation acquired, in him and through him, a marvelous worth, a significance of salvation with a view to eternal life. The Son of God chose to take as his own our human life, our history, our human growth, both physical and spiritual: in the heart of his family—as we are told in Luke—"Jesus advanced in wisdom and age and favor before God and man" (2:52); he "grew and became strong in spirit" (1:80). He grew in his human maturation, in his family relations, and in his preparation for his mission. O precious moments of the life of the Savior! Great missions in the service of man are not improvised; they demand long preparation, in the silence of a tenacious and persevering dedication to hard work.

ANGELUS, PRATO, ITALY
March 19, 1986

Alongside Jesus, you see the sweet depiction of Mary, his Mother and our Mother, you sense the reassuring presence of Joseph, a "righteous" man (Mt 1:19), who earned a living for the entire family in hardworking silence. Today, March nineteenth, it is primarily on him that the eyes of our heart come to rest, to admire the qualities of discretion and generosity, hard work and courage, that surround his gentle figure in a halo of captivating empathy. The whole Christian tradition has viewed Saint Joseph as the patron saint and protector of the community of believers; his powerful intercession accompanies and protects the path of the Church through the course of history.

Have confidence in this saint who is so great and so humble. Participant that he is in the mystery of Mary and of his divine Son, he will gently and safely guide you to an understanding of this mystery of salvation, and he will bring to culmination all the most wonderful things—in the light of God—that your heart desires.

ANGELUS, PRATO, ITALY
March 19, 1986

In contact with the beauty of the mountains, in the presence of the spectacular grandeur of the peaks, the glaciers, and the immense panoramas, man becomes himself again and discovers that the beauty of the universe does not only glow in the marvelous framework of the outer firmament, but rather attains the inner firmament, the firmament of the soul that allows itself to be illuminated and attempts to give meaning to life. From the things that are contemplated, in fact, the spirit is elevated to God in the breath of prayer and gratitude toward the Creator.

SPEECH TO DELEGATES OF THE ITALIAN ALPINE CLUB
April 26, 1986

106

May you be torches that burn in the middle of the world: where there is the night of unbelief, may the light of your faith cast a strong light; where there is the soot of hatred and despair, may the glow of your optimism and hope shine in; where there is the darkness of selfishness and violence, let the fire of your love burn bright.

SPEECH TO YOUTH, IMOLA, ITALY
May 9, 1986

It isn't easy to be Christians nowadays! It's not easy in terms of the faith, because it is necessary to believe everything that Christ revealed and that the Church teaches with its magisterium; it's not easy in terms of moral conduct, because you must obey all the commandments and perform charity, sometimes even with heroic commitment; it's not easy in terms of the example and testimony that you must give to society, in spite of the temptation to fall in line with a worldly mentality.

But Holy Mary is our Mother, teacher, and friend, and she helps us in our difficulties. Mary helps us to have the courage of our faith. She, who lived on faith her whole life, from the Annunciation to Calvary, from Bethlehem to Pentecost, teaches us that the will of God is precisely our faith in Christ, in his Word incarnate and always present in the Church.

SPEECH TO YOUTH, IMOLA, ITALY
May 9, 1986

To wed, for two Christians, is first and foremost an act of faith; it is a way to transfer their human love into the supernatural order, it is an entrusting of their love to God, so that God himself will take it into his care, guaranteeing it with his grace and his benediction. According to the very words of the divine Master, it is not so much that they are joining together, but rather that our Heavenly Father is joining them. And their principal duty will be to not break this union. They will succeed to the degree that they remember that God himself is the guarantor of this union and that therefore, in the difficult moments, they can turn to him with full and limitless faith.

HOLY MASS FOR FAMILIES, FAENZA, ITALY
May 10, 1986

All those for whom pain is a dramatic enigma, which it seems impossible to solve, will find comfort in the example set by Jesus, who drew close to and incessantly placed himself alongside the world of human suffering, taking it upon himself. He, the Innocent One—just as the children who are taken in and cared for here are innocent—illuminates the mystery of suffering with love, which makes pain useful and redeeming. In him, God made suffering and dying an instrument of redemption and the door through which we can enter life without end.

May the grace of God enlarge your hearts, that you may be able to know and understand the profound love of him who is the light and the life for all men. Know that God loves you and is close to you. He deeply understands your tribulations, and your aspirations too. May your faith in him always be a light and a comfort to you.

MEETING WITH INVALIDS, RAVENNA, ITALY
May 11, 1986

What fills Jesus's heart? It is full of love. It is a heart full of love of the Father: full in a way that is divine and at the same time human. In fact, the heart of Jesus is truly the human heart of God the Son. It is therefore full of filial love: everything that he did and said on Earth testifies to precisely that filial love.

At the same time, the filial love of the heart of Jesus has revealed—and continually reveals to the world—the love of the Father. For the Father "so loved the world that he gave his only Son" for the salvation of the world; for the salvation of man, so that he "might not perish but might have eternal life" (Jn 3:16).

The heart of Jesus is therefore full of love for man. It is full of love for the creature. Full of love for the world. How full it is! This fullness is never exhausted. When humanity draws upon the resources of the Earth, the water and the air, these resources diminish and are slowly exhausted. What happens with love is quite otherwise.

ANGELUS
July 13, 1986

Let us look, together with Mary, inside this heart! A patient heart because it is open to all the sufferings of man. A patient heart because it is willing itself to accept a suffering that cannot be measured by any human standards! A patient heart because it is immensely merciful!

Indeed, what is mercy, if not that very particular measure of love that expresses itself in suffering? Indeed, what is mercy, if not that definitive measure of love that descends into the very center of evil to conquer it with good? What is it, if not the love that triumphs over the sin of the world through suffering and death?

Mother, you who by the will of this heart have become the Mother of us all. Who knows as well as you the mystery of the heart of Jesus in Bethlehem, in Nazareth, on Calvary? Who knows as you do that it is patient and immensely merciful? Who renders as you do incessant testimony?

ANGELUS
July 27, 1986

Heart of Jesus, broken because of our sins. Jesus of Nazareth, who during the Last Supper said, "Take, this is my body offered in sacrifice for you. . . . This is my blood of the covenant, which is poured out for you." Jesus: faithful priest who through his own blood enters into the eternal tabernacle; Jesus: priest who, according to the order of Melchizedek, leaves us this sacrifice of his: do this! . . . Heart of Jesus! Heart of Jesus in Gethsemane, who is "sorrowful even to death," who feels the terrible weight. When he says, "Father, all things are possible to you. Take this cup away from me" (Mk 14:36), he knows, at the same time, what the will of his Father is, and he desires nothing but to comply with his will: to drain the goblet to the dregs.

Heart of Jesus—broken with the eternal sentence: For God so loved the world that he gave his only Son.

ANGELUS, CASTEL GANDOLFO, ITALY
August 31, 1986

In the presence of the majestic spectacle of these powerful peaks and these immaculate snows, the mind rises spontaneously to him who is the creator of these wonders: "From eternity to eternity you are God" (Ps 90:2). Throughout time, mankind has considered the mountains to be the site of a privileged experience of God and his incomparable grandeur. The existence of man is precarious and changeable, the existence of mountains is stable and enduring: an eloquent image of the immutable eternity of God. On the mountains, the chaotic noise of the city is no longer heard and what dominates is the silence of boundless space: a silence in which man is permitted to hear more distinctly the interior echo of the voice of God. When we look at mountain peaks we have the impression that the earth is reaching upward as if attempting to reach heaven. In that impetus, man feels that his yearning for the transcendent and the infinite has in some sense found expression.

ANGELUS, AOSTA, ITALY
September 7, 1986

As children of God, and in order to become ever more truly so, we men and women of faith therefore wish to commit ourselves in favor of peace. And we wish to do this together. Yes, our differences are many and profound. Not infrequently in the past, those differences have also been the cause of grievous clashes. Now the Lord helps us to better understand that, beyond our differences and our truths, there is the man, the woman, the children of this world, to whom we would all like to give the best of what we have: our faith that can transform the world. A common faith in God has a fundamental value. By allowing us to recognize all people as creations of God, it helps us to discover universal brotherhood.

ANGELUS
September 28, 1986

Mary, daughter of Israel, you have proclaimed the mercy given to men, from era to era, through the benevolent love of Our Father. Mary, Holy Virgin, servant of the Lord, you have borne in your womb the precious fruit of divine mercy. Mary, you have held safe in your heart the Words of salvation, witnesses before the world of the absolute faithfulness of God to his love. Mary, you who followed your Son Jesus to the very foot of the Cross, in the *fiat* of your heart of a mother, you have subscribed without reservations to the redeeming sacrifice. Mary, Mother of Mercy, show your children the heart of Jesus, which you saw open as an everlasting source of life. Mary, present in the midst of the disciples, you bring us closer to the life-giving love of your risen Son. Mary, Mother attentive to the dangers and the ordeals of the brothers of your Son, do not cease to lead us on the path to salvation.

ANGELUS, PARAY-LE-MONIAL, FRANCE
October 5, 1986

To be friends of Jesus, our Savior and Redeemer! That is the goal for which we should strive. That is the secret of life! Those who are friends of Jesus fear nothing, walk safely, avoid sin, and always improve in their achievement of good. To follow Jesus, to be sure, is not always easy. It demands sacrifice; you must overcome your own whims and selfishness. But it is the greatest joy that ever can be! Jesus doesn't disappoint; he is a loyal friend, who keeps his promises and never forsakes you in times of pain and challenge. But you too must try to be sincere friends to him, doing your best to not cause him sorrow. He wants you to be holy, that is, true and complete Christians, just as other people your age have been, who were born and lived in this city or in other cities in Italy and around the world.

SPEECH TO CHILDREN, FLORENCE, ITALY
October 18, 1986

And what other goal, intrinsic in their existence, do the cultural institutions of the history of man have, if not the pursuit of truth? And what is the most fitting attitude—for men of culture, whether they are teachers or students—for this deeply moving adventure, if not humility? Humility in the sincere quest for truth: humility in accepting it; humility in transmitting it to others.

SPEECH TO FACULTY AND STUDENTS OF THE UNIVERSITY OF PERUGIA
October 26, 1986

Continue, then, to look to the future, trusting that it can become better; indeed, ready yourselves from this moment, conscientiously, to improve it. In the face of this commitment you have the right to expect that this generation of adults—not always generous with the young—will not leave you alone in the legitimate search for a place to apply your skills and willingness to work. Justice and social peace demand this.

But I also feel the need to warn you against a pitfall that can lie concealed inside you young people. It consists of forgetting the tree that God planted in the garden, a tree that marks a limitation to man's will, to the determination to establish, himself, what is good and what is evil. This limitation does not mean—as might be suggested even today by the ever-active demon of an ill-conceived autonomy—that God has any intention of undermining his highest creation. It is rather a reminder of his inborn limits as a creature, his fragility, intended to help him to overcome his tendency toward egocentricity.

ANGELUS FOR UNIVERSITY STUDENTS, PERUGIA, ITALY
October 26, 1986

"Rely on the mighty Lord; constantly seek his face" (Ps 105:4). Every Christian is called upon to give this basic orientation to his life. God, in fact, touches each one of us closely, He touches our conscience and our destiny. To seek him is, all the same, a gratifying effort because he allows us to find him both through the paths of natural knowledge and also, especially, through those of faith and grace.

The most privileged path for such discovery is certainly prayer. Enveloped as we are in the darkness of faith, prayer is the path that leads us to the light, to the full revelation of the God who "is hidden" (Is 45:15). The voice of the psalmist in this connection expresses itself with evocative accents: "O God, you are my God—for you I long! . . . for you my soul thirsts" (Ps 63:2).

ANGELUS
November 16, 1986

In the history of salvation and in the life of each one of us, God is continually taking the initiative, asking us to respond in faith, inviting us to give our consent. It is God who takes the initiative because it is God who directs the course of history. As the Lord says through the prophet Jeremiah: "For I know well the plans I have in mind for you . . . plans for your welfare, not for woe! Plans to give you a future full of hope" (29:11).

ANGELUS, WELLINGTON, NEW ZEALAND
November 23, 1986

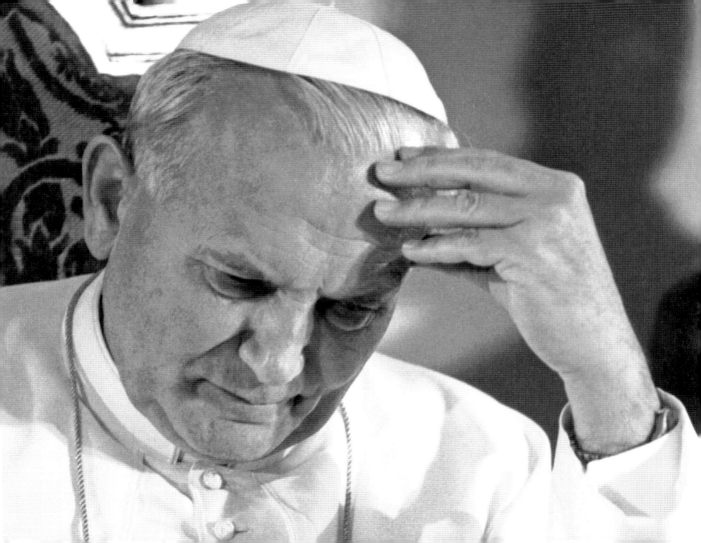

Faith is our source of joy. We believe in a God who created us so that we might enjoy human happiness—in some measure on Earth, in its fullness in heaven. We are meant to have our human joys: the joy of living, the joy of love and friendship, the joy of work well done. We who are Christians have a further cause for joy: like Jesus, we know that we are loved by God our Father. This love transforms our lives and fills us with joy. It makes us see that Jesus did not come to lay burdens upon us. He came to teach us what it means to be fully happy and fully human. Therefore, we discover joy when we discover truth—the truth about God our Father, the truth about Jesus our Savior, the truth about the Holy Spirit who lives in our hearts.

ANGELUS, ADELAIDE, AUSTRALIA
November 30, 1986

We do not pretend that life is all beauty. We are aware of darkness and sin, of poverty and pain. But we know Jesus has conquered sin and passed through his own pain to the glory of the Resurrection. And we live in the light of his Paschal Mystery — the mystery of his Death and Resurrection. "We are an Easter People and Alleluia is our song!" We are not looking for a shallow joy but rather a joy that comes from faith, that grows through unselfish love, that respects the "fundamental duty of love of neighbor, without which it would be unbecoming to speak of joy." We realize that joy is demanding — it demands unselfishness; it demands a readiness to say with Mary: "May it be done to me according to your word."

ANGELUS, ADELAIDE, AUSTRALIA
November 30, 1986

By its nature, music brings men closer to the values of the spirit.

Therefore the Christian religion has found music to be an excellent means of expression. . . . As a universal language, music encourages communion among men of various languages and cultures, and it ennobles the human spirit. Through music is expressed the richness of the cultures of all peoples.

It is well known that the most sublime musical compositions have originated here in Europe and a great many composers took their inspiration specifically from Christianity. Thus the art of music can contribute, in its way, to bringing together and uniting the peoples of Europe who share common Christian roots. Continue then in the future to cultivate assiduously the art of music, enriching with your artistic patrimony the other peoples of Europe. May your music elevate your spirit ever higher toward truth, goodness, and beauty, and toward the values of universal brotherhood.

SPEECH TO THE ACADEMIC CHOIR IVAN GORAN KOVAČIĆ OF ZAGREB
January 17, 1987

It is a wonderful thing, dear boys and girls, to be Christians, to be bearers of Christ. That is how the first generations of Christians thought of themselves in the first centuries and how others thought of them: bearers of Christ, bearers of God, *christophoroi*; in the Greek language, *theophoroi*. Behold: Christ is the light for us, Christ is the light for all mankind. If you are bearers of Christ, you are also bearers of light. That is our task. That is why you must prepare properly; that is what all the life of your parish is directed toward, especially the catechism, the preparation for the sacraments, difficult, no doubt, but rewarding. And I wish to thank for this preparation all of those who exert themselves along with your parish priest: the priests, the nuns, the catechists, all those who take part in this effort to help Jesus Christ to grow in you, because he is the light of the world.

If you are going to gleam like the light of the world, you must have Christ in you, his truth, this truth that is always preached to us, always remembered in the Gospels, this truth that is testified above all with one's life.

SPEECH TO CHILDREN OF SAINT MARY MOTHER OF PROVIDENCE PARISH, ROME, ITALY
February 1, 1987

Dear brothers, may these words of the Lord be for you as well a source of faith and encouragement in your difficulties and dark moments; let them be a guarantee of continual assistance, which he will never deny to anyone who turns to him with faith, to him who holds the keys to all the enigmas of the human heart and who gives ultimate meaning to every action. If, like the apostles, you have Jesus with you on the voyage of your life, you need fear neither tempests nor unfavorable winds. The image of the ship is the symbol of the Church in the world. Saint Augustine, in his journeys to and from Africa, plied the seas and, great thinker that he was, he did not miss the opportunity to express a spiritual reflection in that context: "We are sailors, when we look out at the waves and the tempests of this earthly world. But we do not sink, because we are carried safely by the wood of the cross" (*Treatise on the Gospel of John*, 27:7).

The Church is this life raft of salvation that assures you safe passage, and Christ is the safe harbor, he is the lighthouse that guides and illuminates your navigation.

SPEECH TO LONGSHOREMEN AND FISHERMEN, CIVITAVECCHIA, ITALY
March 19, 1987

What does it mean to be a bridegroom? A bridegroom is he who is aware of the gift. We have seen how Joseph of Nazareth, a simple man, was aware of the divine gift. But divine gifts proliferate throughout all of reality: they are the gifts of creation, of grace, of the human person. The human person is a special gift of the Creator and the Redeemer together. Indeed, to be a bridegroom is to be aware of the gift. This awareness creates a new mentality, a new attitude, a new behavior; when we see the gift in the works of creation and above all in people. Thus, Saint Joseph clearly saw with the eyes of his dignity and faith the gift of the person of Mary, the ineffable gift of the person of his divine Son.

SPEECH TO YOUTH, CIVITAVECCHIA, ITALY
March 19, 1987

During the years of Jesus's hidden life in the house at Nazareth, Mary's life too is "hid with Christ in God" (cf. Col 3:3) through faith. For faith is contact with the mystery of God. Every day Mary is in constant contact with the ineffable mystery of God-made man, a mystery that surpasses everything revealed in the Old Covenant. From the moment of the Annunciation, the mind of the Virgin-Mother has been initiated into the radical "newness" of God's self-revelation and has been made aware of the mystery. She is the first of those "little ones" of whom Jesus will say one day: "Father, . . . although you have hidden these things from the wise and the learned you have revealed them to the childlike" (Mt 11:25).

ENCYCLICAL REDEMPTORIS MATER, § 17
March 25, 1987

Beloved campesinos: your work has a special nobility because it constitutes an essential service, invaluable to the entire community, and because, through it, you achieve your human vocation as collaborators of God, in close contact with nature.

Precisely because work is a collaboration with God, we Christians cannot be satisfied with work done by halves. The "gospel of work" that Jesus of Nazareth taught us during his life as a carpenter should inspire you in your own tasks, should spur you also to improve your own culture and to perfect your professional skills.

GREETING TO CAMPESINOS, MAIPÚ, CHILE
April 3, 1987

Never tire of learning more about the Mother of God, who is also our Mother, and above all never tire of imitating her in her complete compliance with the will of God, with the sole concern of pleasing her and never causing her sadness.

You know that it is necessary to pray, and you must do so while considering and remembering all that Jesus did and suffered for us: the mysteries of his childhood, his Passion and Death, and his glorious Resurrection.

When you recite your "mystery" or "decade," you follow the inspiration of the Holy Spirit, which, by instructing you internally, leads you to imitate more closely Jesus, allowing you to pray with Mary and, most important, like Mary. It is a great contemplative prayer, very useful to the people of today who are also so busy with so many things; it is the proper prayer for Mary and her devoted followers.

SPEECH TO CHILDREN OF THE LIVING ROSARY
April 25, 1987

The relief of suffering! In this sweet expression is summarized one of the essential prospects of Christian charity, of that fraternal charity that Christ taught us and which, by his express admonition, is and must be the distinctive sign of his disciples; of that charity whose material implementation, especially toward the neediest, is a crucial factor of credibility in that message of truth, love, and salvation that the Christian is expected to announce to the world. This work for which Padre Pio prayed so fervently and worked so tirelessly is a magnificent testament to Christian love.

Padre Pio's great intuition was to bring science in the service of the ill, together with faith and prayer: medical science in the increasingly advanced battle against disease; faith and prayer in transfiguring and exalting the suffering that, despite all the progress of medicine, will always remain, to a certain degree, the heritage of life on Earth.

SPEECH TO DOCTORS AND PATIENTS OF THE HOME FOR RELIEF OF THE SUFFERING,
SAN GIOVANNI ROTONDO, ITALY
May 23, 1987

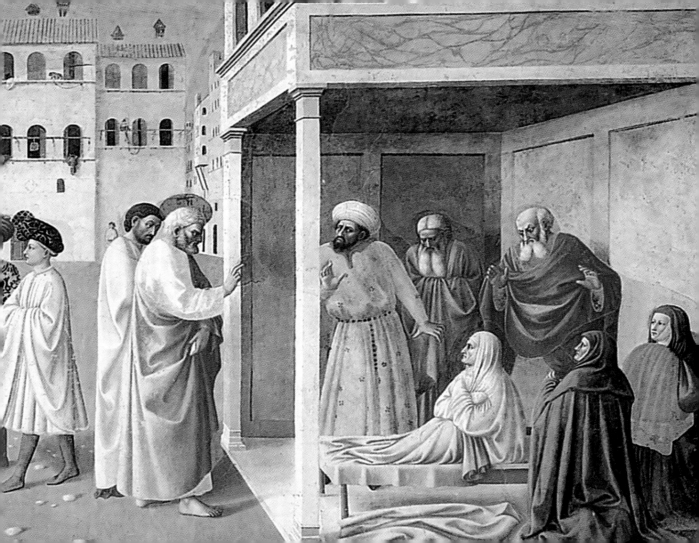

Beloved husbands and wives, who have been living in your conjugal union for so many years; fiancées and fiancés, who are preparing to consecrate your reciprocal love in the sacrament! A family has the mission of becoming increasingly what it is in the plans of God, that is to say, a community of life and love; it therefore has the mission of protecting, revealing, and communicating, in unity and indissolubility, life and love, as reflections of their participation in God's love for mankind and Christ's love for the Church, his bride. Without authentic reciprocal love, the family cannot live, cannot grow, cannot perfect itself as a community of people: it is this love that leads to the gift of life to the children and leads to solidarity and communion with other families. All of this demands a great spirit of sacrifice; generous willingness to offer understanding, forgiveness, and reconciliation; preventing selfishness, conflict, and tensions from lurking in the family community.

SPEECH TO FAMILIES, FOGGIA, ITALY
May 24, 1987

To educate one's children to the great values of the Christian faith; to a faith in God the Father, in Christ his Son, and in the Holy Spirit! The first school of catechism is and must be the family! From the father and the mother, from the older brothers and sisters the little children must receive—along with examples of Christian life—the treasure of the great truths of the Divine Revelation, which they will later study in greater depth with the organic catechism in the parish churches, in the institutions, and in the movements.

Most important of all, however, you parents must educate your children in prayer, introduce them to the progressive discovery of the mystery of God and to personal conversation with him. This prayer conducted within the family, which is the domestic church, constitutes for the children the natural introduction to the liturgical prayer of the entire Church. There is then a progressive participation of all the members of the Christian family in the Eucharist, especially on Sundays and holidays, and the other sacraments, in particular those of Christian initiation.

SPEECH TO FAMILIES, FOGGIA, ITALY
May 24, 1987

There are those who may ask, "O Lord, why? Why all this?" It is the perennial question that the greatest minds have labored over, without being able to come up with an explanation. The problem of evil in general and of natural calamities in particular remains a dense mystery, utterly senseless to the human intellect. The only support upon which man can rely is the thought that God is never indifferent to the suffering of his children, but involved himself dramatically in the person of his only Son, Jesus Christ, who was subject to "our weaknesses, . . . who has similarly been tested in every way" (Heb 4:15).

SPEECH TO SURVIVORS OF THE VAJONT DAM CATASTROPHE, FORTOGNA DI LONGARONE, ITALY
July 2, 1987

Every Christian is, in fact, essentially an apostle. This noble status obliges him to undertake any and all efforts, personally and as part of a community, to achieve that which we invoke when we pray: "Your kingdom come." The human being is endowed with a sociable nature. With baptism, then, he forms part of the people of God and becomes a member of the mystical body of Christ, so that his natural sociability is fulfilled by a community bond of a superior nature.

ANGELUS
August 2, 1987

It is with the truth of Jesus, dear young people, that you must face the great questions in your lives, as well as the practical problems. The world will try to deceive you about many things that matter: about your faith, about pleasure and material things, about the dangers of drugs. And at one stage or another the false voices of the world will try to exploit your human weakness by telling you that life has no meaning at all for you. The supreme theft in your lives would be if they succeeded in robbing you of hope. They will try, but not succeed if you hold fast to Jesus and his truth.

The truth of Jesus is capable of reinforcing all your energies. It will unify your lives and consolidate your sense of mission. You may still be vulnerable to attack from the pressures of the world, from the forces of evil, from the power of the devil. But you will be invincible in hope: in "Christ Jesus our hope" (1 Tim 1:1).

Dear young people: the word of Jesus and his truth and his promises of fulfillment and life are the Church's response to the culture of death, to the onslaughts of doubt, and to the cancer of despair.

SPEECH TO YOUTH, NEW ORLEANS, LOUISIANA
September 12, 1987

What does it mean to educate? Educating means making a human being more humane, making his humanity more profound, creating an authentically human personality and, for a Christian, forming a Christian personality. This is the objective and the task of this community, the school, the class in which you are present and involved. Working together with those who educate you means cooperating with your parents. To receive education at school means for you to cooperate with your teachers. Your teacher is very pleased with what I am now telling you. You should cooperate with her. This is very important, inasmuch as it gives meaning to our life; and so we are active in building ourselves, each of us; cooperating with our parents, our teachers, with the Church and society, and in this way, with God himself. This is the profound meaning of the words that you have often heard: that we were created in God's image. This image of God in each of us is marvelous, but it must be created, it must be created by us ourselves and through education, together with the parents, the teachers, and so on.

SPEECH TO STUDENTS AT THE IMMACULATE CONCEPTION SCHOOL, LOS ANGELES, CALIFORNIA
September 16, 1987

The holiness of the family is the thoroughfare and the obligatory path for the construction of a new and better society, to give renewed hope in the future to a world that is menaced by so many threats. May the Christian families of today, then, enroll in the school of that center of love and unfettered giving that was the Holy Family. The Son of God, having become small, like all those who are born of woman, received the constant care of the Mother. Mary, who was still a virgin, consecrated her life daily to the sublime mission of maternity, and for this reason too all people nowadays call her blessed. Joseph, designated to protect the mystery of the divine filiality of Jesus and the maternal virginity of Mary, played his role, in complete awareness, in silence and obedience to divine will. What a school, what a mystery!

ANGELUS, CASTEL GANDOLFO, ITALY
December 27, 1987

Mary is the morning star that precedes the dawn and the sun of justice, Christ our Lord. Even before Jesus spoke of himself and his mission, Mary spoke of him to those who came to visit the child, and who were astonished and amazed to learn what God had done for the salvation of Israel and all of mankind. Mary is the star of the sea. Her faith is like the light that guides us through the crashing waves and the tempests of this world, and that illuminates the shadows of our ignorance, dissipating error and leading us to the truth, which is Christ. Mary is like the star of Bethlehem, which showed the location of the Son of God, come down among us, to free man from death and sin and to make him the Son of God. Mary, like the star of Bethlehem, leads everyone to Christ from near and far, both those who belong to Israel and those who do not; both those who already believe, in order to help them to believe even more, and those who do not yet believe, in order that they might finally attain faith.

ANGELUS
January 6, 1988

Blessed is the husband who, like Saint Joseph, manifests his love by earning a living for the household with the work of his hands. "What your hands provide you will enjoy; you will be happy and prosper" the psalm tells us (128:2).

Blessed is the wife whose maternity is compared by the psalmist to "a fruitful vine," woman and mother, heart of the family, who truly represents the intimacy of your house (Ps 128:3) and around whom everyone gathers, attracted by her caring love. The woman like Mary, with her love and her work, hidden and generous, gives substance to the household hearth.

Blessed are the children — in the words of the psalm — who from babyhood grow in the family "like olive plants." Not only "around your table" (Ps 128:3), but also and especially around the parents, who should be the best model of how to grow in wisdom and grace, like Jesus of Nazareth.

Blessed, last of all, is the society that makes possible the fitting growth of its families, that encourages the serene and fertile development of the vocation of everyone within the family.

HOLY MASS FOR FAMILIES, LA PAZ, BOLIVIA
May 10, 1988

Do not hesitate to turn to Jesus. Turn to him once you see his face: it is not the face of a prophet, not the face of a wise man or a liberator, but the face of God-made man. The Lord will not ask you to perform great deeds, but simply the quotidian effort of contributing day after day to the construction of your fatherland through a competent professional preparation, the unselfish performance of work in relation to others—without giving in to "slacking"—while serving your brothers on a thousand small everyday occasions.

MEETING WITH YOUTH, COCHABAMBA, BOLIVIA
May 11, 1988

Men of yesterday and today, tell us: what can our century hand down to posterity, if somewhere in the world today there still persists the system of the death camps?

Tell us, were we not too quick to forget your hell? Do we not efface from our memories and from our consciousness the traces of past misdeeds?

Tell us, which direction should Europe and mankind take after Auschwitz, after Mauthausen? Is the direction in which we are moving away from those horrible experiences of the past the correct one?

Tell us, what should men of today be like, what should the generations be like who live on the ruins of this immense defeat of humanity?

What should man be like? What should he demand from himself?

Tell us, how should the nations and the societies be? How should Europe proceed to live?

Speak, because you have the right—you who have suffered and lost your life. . . . Speak, and we have the duty to listen to your testimony.

MEETING WITH CONCENTRATION CAMP SURVIVORS, MAUTHAUSEN, AUSTRIA
June 24, 1988

Motherhood involves a special communion with the mystery of life, as it develops in the woman's womb. The mother is filled with wonder at this mystery of life, and "understands" with unique intuition what is happening inside her. In the light of the "beginning," the mother accepts and loves as a person the child she is carrying in her womb. This unique contact with the new human being developing within her gives rise to an attitude toward human beings—not only toward her own child, but every human being—which profoundly marks the woman's personality. It is commonly thought that women are more capable than men of paying attention to another person and that motherhood develops this predisposition even more. The man—even with all his sharing in parenthood—always remains "outside" the process of pregnancy and the baby's birth; in many ways he has to learn his own "fatherhood" from the mother.

APOSTOLIC LETTER MULIERIS DIGNITATEM, § 18
August 15, 1988

The moral and spiritual strength of a woman is joined to her awareness that God entrusts the human being to her in a special way. Of course, God entrusts every human being to each and every other human being. But this entrusting concerns women in a special way—precisely by reason of their femininity—and this in a particular way determines their vocation.

A woman is strong because of her awareness of this entrusting, strong because of the fact that God "entrusts the human being to her," always and in every way, even in the situations of social discrimination in which she may find herself. This awareness and this fundamental vocation speak to women of the dignity, which they receive from God himself, and this makes them "strong" and strengthens their vocation. Thus the "perfect woman" (cf. Prv 31:10) becomes an irreplaceable support and source of spiritual strength for other people, who perceive the great energies of her spirit. These "perfect women" are owed much by their families, and sometimes by whole nations.

APOSTOLIC LETTER MULIERIS DIGNITATEM, § 30
August 15, 1988

And so this is my wish to you this evening: may you be fervent, convinced, and open to hope.

But all this would remain nothing more than a vain dream, a vague ambition, if there were not a specific reference to Christ. He is the light; he is the way and the truth; he is the life, because he has reconciled us with the Father and has donated himself as the bread of life.

Live on him then! And this, with the convinced, constant, and joyous participation in the Sunday Eucharist, nourishing yourself frequently on his body and his blood, the only support of our earthly journey.

And if, as you travel the roads of the world, you happen sometimes to stumble and fall, turn to him, who in the sacrament of Penitence will be waiting for you with open arms on the Cross, and he will bestow upon you once again forgiveness, serenity of heart, and joy in living. Say confession often, and confess yourself well!

SPEECH TO YOUTH AT THE CONFRONTO '88 RALLY, TURIN, ITALY
September 2, 1988

What is needed in today's world is "a civilization of love," a kind of atmosphere in which the human mind thinks thoughts of peace and rejects the option of violence, where the heart is drawn to beauty and goodness and to the urgent needs of others, where people join hands as brothers and sisters to labor in solidarity for the rights and dignity of all, especially for the poorest and most defenseless members of society.

Yes, "a man can have no greater love than to lay down his life for his friends." That is the key to understand the life of Jesus Christ and of his faithful followers of every time and place. It is an accurate description of Blessed Joseph Gérard during the many years that he lived in this land. And even for those who do not believe in the Christian faith, these words about love ring true. For love is the most powerful force for changing the face of the Earth.

FAREWELL SPEECH, MASERU, LESOTHO
September 16, 1988

To be young is already in itself a special and specific treasure for every young man and young woman. This treasure consists, among other things, in the fact that yours is an age of many important discoveries. Each one of you discovers him- or herself, his or her personality, the meaning for him or for her of existence, the reality of good and evil. You also discover the whole world around you – the human world and the world of nature. Now, among these many discoveries there must not be lacking one that is of fundamental importance for every human being: the personal discovery of Jesus Christ. Discovering Christ, always again and always more fully, is the most wonderful adventure of our life.

MESSAGE FOR WORLD YOUTH DAY IV
November 27, 1988

We young people, if we wish to give an answer to Christ, to his proposal, to his "follow me," must pass through this central mystery, this central reality: to know Jesus, to know God, and to know oneself with the key to this mystery.

The answer "follow me" is simple and, at the same time, immensely rich. In this answer we can find the entire reality of a vocation, especially the basic observation that man, the human person, is a being who has a vocation, who has a profound purpose to his existence, to his being, for which it is worthwhile to engage oneself, for which it is worthwhile to live. This is already something of enormous importance, because so many of our contemporaries suffer precisely over this question, suffer from the lack of an answer: Why live? What is the meaning of our lives? Of our efforts? Of our sufferings?

Every human being carries a divine calling etched on the heart: my life is not in vain. God predestined us to live in Christ, to live for all eternity the fullness of divine life through Christ in the Holy Spirit. This God already inscribes in our being an earthly vocation that is Christian.

SPEECH TO ROMAN YOUTH, WORLD YOUTH DAY IV
March 18, 1989

Young people and Easter: Isn't there a particularly close tie between these two? Isn't the younger generation a special "place" for the event of Easter? How could we fail to see in youth and its values—life, health, beauty, physical vigor, enthusiasm, joy—almost a precursor to the triumph of Christ risen and his glorious return? What a commitment, then, for you young people, to live more intensely, above all, the victory over sin, obtained through Easter, that victory over evil, of which your inner lives and your very physical appearance are such a lovely symbol!

ANGELUS
March 19, 1989

Already I hear the questions you want to ask me: How can we become saints if there are so many obstacles in our way? How can we be honest if there is bribery and corruption around us? How can we become holy if the surest way to earn a living is to be mean and to exploit others? How can we become holy if we live in a world that cheapens true love or does not appreciate the beauty of chaste love? I hear these questions and many more besides. God the Father knows your difficulties, but he also knows that deep down you want to do the right thing; deep down you want to follow Christ because you know that he is "the way and the truth and the life" (Jn 14:6).

Of course, the path to holiness is not easy, but that should not prevent us from facing the difficulties with courage. The path to holiness is a journey, sometimes a difficult journey involving an inner struggle against selfishness and sin. We must be properly equipped to make this journey. Saint Paul gives us a list of the "clothing" – the attitudes – necessary: "heartfelt compassion, kindness, humility, gentleness, and patience" (Col 3:12).

SPEECH TO YOUTH, BLANTYRE, MALAWI
May 5, 1989

A worker—every one of you, I mean to say—is not a mechanism in a factory, nor is he a tool with which to do work: he belongs to an order of greatness superior to all material realities that exist within our visible horizon. He is a being endowed, by his nature, with intelligence and liberty: in a word, he is a person. And every human person, without any discrimination, is made in the image of God the Creator. His dignity, therefore, outweighs the value of all earthly goods.

But there is more: a worker is called by God to fit in with his plan of Creation and to become, in a certain sense, a creator himself.

From this there derives an immediate and important consequence: whatever the level at which he operates or the category to which he belongs, a worker pursing his activity must be able to become more human, and therefore not be degraded or humiliated as a result of that work.

SPEECH TO ENTREPRENEURS AND WORKERS, GROSSETO, ITALY
May 21, 1989

Tenderness, as a sincerely filial attitude toward God, is expressed in prayer. The experience of one's own existential poverty, of the void that earthly things leave in the soul, arouses in man the need to turn to God to obtain grace, help, and forgiveness. The gift of piety guides and encourages this need, enriching it with sentiments of profound faith toward God, perceived as a good and provident Father. It was in this sense that Saint Paul wrote: "God sent his Son . . . to ransom those under the law, so that we might receive adoption. As proof that you are children, God sent the spirit of his Son into our hearts, crying out, 'Abba, Father!' So you are no longer a slave but a child" (Gal 4:4–7).

ANGELUS
May 28, 1989

Blessed Mary, look with kindness today upon every home. Obtain for families the joy and harmony that filled the house at Nazareth. Unite parents in faithful love, and bless all children. Help young adults to respond generously and faithfully to Christ. Teach everyone the value of forgiveness and fraternal love.

O Mother of Mercy, comfort the elderly and the sick. Help the injured and handicapped. Assist those who suffer from cancer, AIDS, or any incurable illness. Give hope and fresh courage to all who are afraid, depressed, lost, or unwanted.

Touch the hearts of all who have given up the faith. Call them home! Tell them that the Father loves them and waits for them with open arms. Tell them the Church needs them!

ANGELUS, REYKJAVÍK, ICELAND
June 4, 1989

How can I be blessed? you ask yourself. For the most part, modern society idolizes health, youth, power, and beauty. The sick and the old seem to lack precisely those things that the world so much admires. But there is a higher wisdom, a wisdom that reveals the true meaning of our human weakness and our pain. That wisdom is revealed in Christ. He knows what it is to suffer; he experienced it on the road to Calvary. He was scourged and crowned with thorns; he had to carry the Cross and was crucified.

Christ associates with himself in the closest possible way to all those who suffer. If any of your relatives, neighbors, and those looking after you do not fully understand how much you suffer, be assured that Christ the Lord does. Not only does the Lord understand our sufferings but he teaches us that suffering, pain, growing old, and death itself—all these things have an immense value when they are united with his own Passion and Death. In fact, Jesus says that no one can claim to follow him without taking up his Cross.

MEETING WITH THE ELDERLY AND THE SICK, HELSINKI, FINLAND
June 6, 1989

One of you wrote to me: "What could I ask of my Pope? I could ask him for many things . . . but what? . . . I have the love of my mother, the understanding of my father, in short, the affection of my family. . . . What else could I ask for?"

I would first of all like to tell this young man how grateful he should be to God for the gift of a united family and for this experience of authentic love that he is thus privileged to enjoy. A successful family is not the result of chance, of improvisation. It springs from the generous commitment of all its members: not only from the commitment of your parents, dear young people, but also from your own. You should therefore consider yourselves to be responsible for your respective families. This, above all, is the most serious way of preparing yourselves for the future when you will form a family of your own, harmonious and serene.

I would like, however, to further say to my unidentified interlocutor that a successful family is a great deal, but it is not yet all. God in his goodness offered us the possibility of becoming part of his own family, becoming his children and acquiring in Christ a vast multitude of brothers. This, then, is the "what else" this young person can and should ask for: to be able to be a worthy and active member of the great family of the children of God.

MESSAGE TO THE NEW GENERATIONS, FORMIA, ITALY
June 25, 1989

Peter was personally acquainted with the Mother of Jesus, and in talking with her, especially in the days of reflection while awaiting Pentecost, he was able to deepen his understanding of the mystery of Christ. Paul, announcing the attainment of the plan of salvation "in the fullness of time," did not neglect to mention the "woman" of whom the Son of God had been born into time (cf. Gal 4:4). Knowing how long-standing the veneration of Mary is in Rome, how could we fail to see in the evangelization undertaken by the two apostles in the Eternal City the earliest roots of that singular piety toward the Virgin, "Salus Populi Romani," a piety that is age-old in this city?

ANGELUS
June 29, 1989

The Spirit has shaped the holy humanity of Christ: his body and his soul with all his intelligence, will, and capacity for love. In a word, it has shaped his heart. The life of Christ has been placed under the sign of the Spirit. It is from the Spirit that he obtained the knowledge that astounded the doctors of the law and his fellow citizens, the love that accepts and forgives sinners, the mercy that reaches down toward the misery of man, the tenderness that blesses and embraces the children, and the understanding that soothes the pain of the afflicted. It is the Spirit that guided Jesus's footsteps, that upheld him in his ordeals, and especially that led him on the road to Jerusalem, where he would offer the sacrifice of the new covenant, through which the fire that he brought to Earth would flare up and spread.

ANGELUS
July 2, 1989

The expression "Heart of Jesus" immediately brings to mind the humanity of Christ and emphasizes the richness of his sentiments; his compassion for the sick and halt; his love of the poor; his mercy toward sinners; his tenderness toward children; his strength in denouncing hypocrisy, pride, and violence; his mildness in the face of his opponents; his fervor for the glory of the Father; and his jubilation over God's designs of grace, mysterious and provident.

In reference to the events of the Passion, the expression "Heart of Jesus" also evokes Christ's sorrow over the betrayal by Judas, his dejection over his solitude, his anguish in the face of death, his obedient and filial resignation to the will of his Father. And above all it speaks to the love that pours unstoppably from his inner self: infinite love toward the Father and boundless love toward man.

ANGELUS
July 9, 1989

And so, when he entered the world, Christ said, "Behold, I come to do your will, O God" (Heb 10:5–7). "Obedience" is the new name of "love"!

Over the course of his life, the Gospels portray Jesus as always intent on performing the will of the Father. To Mary and Joseph who searched for him in desperation for three days, the twelve-year-old Jesus responded, "Why were you looking for me? Did you not know that I must be in my Father's house?" (Lk 2:49). His whole life was dominated by this "I must," which guided his choices and directed his activity. He told the disciples one day: "My food is to do the will of the one who sent me and to complete his work" (Jn 4:34); and he taught them to pray with these words: "Our Father . . . your will be done, on earth as in heaven" (Mt 6:10).

ANGELUS
July 23, 1989

The pierced Heart of Jesus is a sign of the totality of this love in a vertical and horizontal direction, like the two arms of the Cross. The pierced Heart is also a symbol of new life, given to men through the Spirit and the sacraments. As soon as the soldier dealt the blow with his spear, from Christ's wounded side "blood and water flowed out" (Jn 19:34). The Evangelist reminds everyone of the stark certainty of the reality. But, at the same time, he tends to delve into the significance of the salvifical event and express it through a symbol. He thus sees a profound significance in the episode of the spear thrust: just as Moses struck a rock in the desert and water gushed out, similarly from Christ's side, pierced by the spear, a torrent of water gushed forth to quench the thirst of the new People of God. This torrent is the gift of the Spirit, which feeds divine life in us.

ANGELUS
July 30, 1989

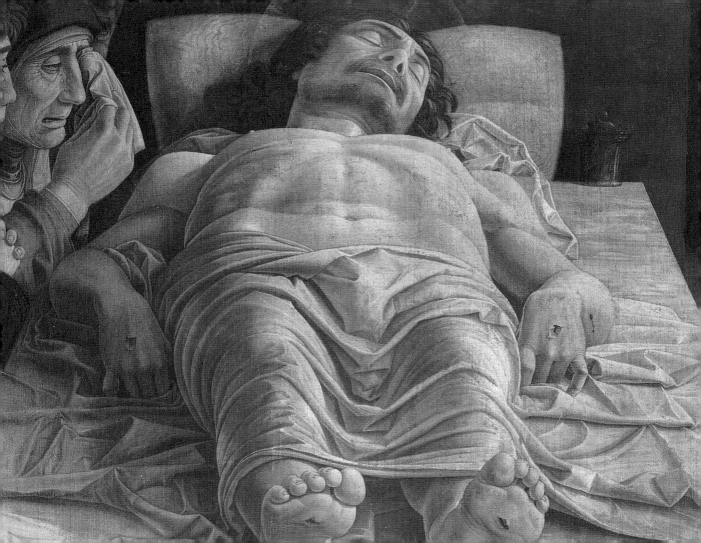

You, young people who have experienced the tragedy of drug addiction, and you, young people who offer alternative models of personal and family self-fulfillment in the courageous decision to engage in volunteer work, you are clearly demonstrating that drugs can be fought not only with health and law-enforcement measures but also—and primarily—by establishing new human relationships, rich in spiritual and emotional values. It is only in this way, in fact, that we can restore full meaning to life, by rousing in those who are in difficulty a renewed enthusiasm in the daily struggle and by reviving in them faith in the final victory.

The models that you establish for yourselves—of welcoming and listening, as they are experienced here in your centers, and of shared responsibility and collaboration, typical of your communities—are valid models, because they are capable of guiding us toward decisions and attitudes inspired by the evangelic values of poverty, service, and sharing; they prove that it is possible to help those who want to conquer drugs, and to set up effective barriers to the societal expansion of this phenomenon.

VISIT TO THE ITALIAN CENTER FOR SOLIDARITY, LUCCA, ITALY
September 23, 1989

For you, young Christians, there should be no doubt: Jesus Christ makes true peace by the blood of the Cross. It is precisely on the Cross that he shows clearly that love is stronger than hatred and violence, forgiveness is more just than retribution. This is not weakness or mere passivism. Your martyrs, many of them of your own age, were much stronger in their suffering and death than their persecutors in their hatred and violence. Violence destroys; love transforms and builds up. This is the challenge that Christ offers to you, young people of Korea, who wish to be instruments of true progress in the history of your country. Christ calls you, not to tear down and destroy, but to transform and build up!

Your hearts suffer when you hear talk of war, when you see the sick, the poor, those who suffer from hunger, and orphaned children. Pray with me for peace, for an end to suffering, for the healing of wounds. But in this, too, I ask you to begin constructing peace yourselves, in the place where you happen to be; as you grow up, become workers on behalf of peace; know that Jesus said they are blessed and will be happy!

You have called me a "pilgrim of peace." I would like to be one wherever I go, because Jesus, in the moment when he was about to give his own life for the world, gave us the profound peace that never left his heart, brimming over with love, his heart of the Son of God and brother to men.

MEETING WITH CHILDREN, CUREPIPE, MAURITIUS
October 16, 1989

Turning my thoughts to you now, beloved old people and invalids, I express to you my deep understanding for your sufferings and I assure you that I remember you always in my prayers. I also want to urge you always to be serene and faithful, knowing full well that the entire history of mankind forms part of a design of love, eternal and providential, by the Father. All suffering, however dolorous and difficult to withstand, finds in the Easter of Christ its salvific function. Disease is a wise teacher for all men! Trust, then, always in the Spirit of the Lord and in the Most Holy Mary! May the recital of the Rosary accompany and console you! Pray also for the Church, for the clergy, and for priests' and nuns' vocations! Pray for all of mankind!

SPEECH TO PATIENTS AND STAFF OF THE CITADEL OF CHARITY, TARANTO, ITALY
October 28, 1989

With marriage, beloved newlyweds, you have undertaken the implementation of a great enterprise: to merge your persons into a single flesh and give birth, out of this magnificent union, to life, the life of man. You are collaborators with the Creator in the diffusion and education of human life. Nuptial love culminates by its nature in paternal and maternal love. Your paternal being and maternal being, all the same—as you know—goes well beyond the simple physical fact, and becomes a form of spiritual generation. And that is where your educational efforts come in! You are summoned to communicate to the fruit of your union not only material goods, but also those goods of the spirit and those virtues, those ideals and moral values that constitute the most precious inheritance. For that inheritance your children will be most grateful. The inheritance of material possessions, however important, can be stolen by a thief or consumed by moths; the inheritance of a life made up of right and holy actions is a treasure that no thief can steal and no moth can consume.

MEETING WITH NEWLYWED COUPLES, TARANTO, ITALY
October 28, 1989

Become courageous defenders of this announcement that liberates the family, all families! Be ready to overcome, with determination, all the forms of discrimination and inequality, mistreatment, scorn, and neglect to the dignity of wives, of children, of minors! Testify, in a clear and unmistakable manner, the respect that you have for life, committing yourself to protect it, from its very beginning, and rejecting all forms of apathy or neglect toward the littlest ones!

Your household hearths, your nuclear families should constitute an example of welcoming, of love and service, as is proper to a Christian family. Do all that you are able to ensure that the family is seen as the fundamental core of society and its existence. And that everyone, beginning with the public authorities and the laws of the community, should respect the family's natural rights!

HOLY MASS, BISSAU, GUINEA-BISSAU
January 27, 1990

To you, man, who look complacently upon the works of your own hand, the fruit of your genius, Christ says: Do not forget him who gave origin to everything!

Do not forget the Creator—Christ tells us—and respect Creation! Perform your work by using properly the resources that God has bestowed upon you! Transform his riches with the aid of science and technology, but do not squander them, do not be a heedless usurper or exploiter of the goods created! Neither destroy nor contaminate! Remember your neighbor, remember the poor! Think of future generations!

Christ says this in particular to the men of our times, who are increasingly aware of the inescapable need to protect the environment that surrounds us.

With what love the eyes of the Master and Redeemer look upon the beauty of the created world! The visible world was created for man. Christ tells those who listen to him: Are you not more worthy than the birds of the sky and the lilies of the field (cf. Mt 6:26, 28)?

Of course the economic, political, and social dimensions of life require careful attention and forthright commitment on the part of all. But at the same time it is necessary to reaffirm adamantly the primacy of ethics over technology, the primacy of "being" over "having." This is especially imperative when we are immersed in a false culture of "appearances," the result of an unbridled consumer mentality detrimental to the deepest needs of individuals and communities. The present challenge facing Europe is to rediscover its own deepest roots. In accepting this challenge, European culture is forcefully called to account for the Christian faith that gave form to its peoples.

SPEECH TO MEMBERS OF SCIENTIFIC, CULTURAL, AND ARTISTIC CIRCLES, SLIEMA, MALTA
May 27, 1990

Dear brothers, we must become usable soil without thorns or stones, but well plowed and carefully hoed and weeded. It is incumbent upon us to be that "good soil" in which "some seed fell . . . and produced fruit, a hundred or sixty or thirtyfold" (Mt 13:8). How great, then, is the responsibility of the believer! How numerous are the opportunities offered to those who accept and preserve this mystery! Blessed are those who open themselves fully to Christ, the seed that fertilizes life!

I exhort you, my dear brothers and sisters, to grow in the desire of God. I encourage you to accept generously the invitation that today's liturgy extends to us. May you always accede to the impulses of grace and bear abundant fruit of holiness.

I would like to say to all of you here today, but especially to the students, that it is a wonderful thing to be a student. This may not fit in with the desire of so many students to stop being students, to change their condition, to be free of examinations. I tell you this by way of consolation, based on my own experience. It is true that it might be preferable to have one's examinations behind one, but on the other hand it is also true, and this is borne out by the experience of those who have already been a student, as I have, that you never really stop being a student. You remain a student for the rest of your life. And throughout your life you will also have to take examinations. I tell you this to console you, because to find oneself still a student, even at my age, for instance, in quite advanced years, gives us joy. It takes us back to the years of youth when we really were students. I would like to address these words to all those who are present, to all the students of the university, wishing them excellent results in their university exams, as well as in all the exams that await them in life.

SPEECH TO THE STUDENTS OF UNIVERSITY OF FERRARA
September 23, 1990

Mother of the Church and our Mother, we hold in our hands everything that a people is capable of offering you: the innocence of the children, the generosity and the enthusiasm of the young, the suffering of the sick, the most genuine affections cultivated within families, the hard work of the laborers, the hardships of the unemployed, the loneliness of the elderly, the anguish of those who seek the true meaning of life, the sincere repentance of those who are lost in sin, the good intentions and the hopes of those who discover the love of the Father, the faithfulness and dedication of those who, having been called to the priesthood or the religious life, expend their energy in the apostolate and in works of mercy.

ACT OF ENTRUSTMENT TO OUR LADY OF THE WATCH, CERANESI, ITALY
October 14, 1990

It is, in fact, this person, deserving of esteem and respect, who entrusts his suffering body to the care of health professionals, placing his full trust in the quality of your medical equipment. Your profession entails a genuine expression of charity and compassion. All this is praiseworthy, and I urge you to draw upon all your knowledge and to depend upon your generosity of spirit and delicacy of sentiment. I encourage you to impart a profoundly human character to your business dealings, both with the hospital personnel and with the sick themselves, while transcending the purely technical aspects and taking inspiration from your keen sense of man, the fruit of evangelical love.

SPEECH TO THE EXECUTIVES OF LABORATOIRES SURGIKOS-FRANCE
January 18, 1991

Hear the unanimous cry of your children,
the heartfelt supplication of all mankind:
never again war, adventure with no return,
never again war, spiral of sorrows and violence;
put an end to this war in the Persian Gulf,
a threat to your creatures, in the sky, on land, and at sea.

In communion with Mary, Mother of Jesus,
again we implore you:
speak to the hearts of those responsible for the destiny of peoples,
end the cycle of revenge and vendetta,
suggest new solutions with your Spirit,
generous and honorable gestures, room for dialogue and patient waiting
more fruitful than the hasty deadlines of war.

PRAYER FOR PEACE
February 2, 1991

The "champion," as we say nowadays, easily becomes a guiding image upon which young people frequently project their own aspirations. It has been said that the visions and the social operations of a generation can be found practically codified in sports, especially in the most popular and widely practiced sports. The athletic tradition, therefore, forms one of the components of a community's culture and, as a result, enters into the formative process of the younger generations.

In this context may you be, especially you athletes, exemplars of values, of those values that underlie ethical choices and that guide the steps and the measures of man toward noble ideals.

In particular, may you be teachers of life lessons for young people, role models upon which they can base their plans for the future. Do not yield to the temptation of a utilitarian vision of life. Work to ensure that many can recognize in you and in your behavior authenticity and rectitude in every challenge.

SPEECH TO THE MANAGERS AND PLAYERS OF THE SOCCER CLUB INTER CALCIO
February 16, 1991

Those who work in the public sector must be especially vigilant with respect to those negative situations that, in the encyclical *Sollicitudo rei socialis*, speaking globally, I described as "structures of sin" (§ 36). They are, in a sense, the sum of the factors that act contrary to the achievement of the common good and respect for the dignity of the individual. One yields to those temptations when, for instance, one seeks only exclusive personal profit or the benefit of a group rather than thinking of the interests of all; when the laws of patronage overwhelm the proper operation of administrative justice; when an excessive attachment to power, in fact, bars the way to new generations; when the political parties, focused solely on their narrow interest, avoid all forms cooperation and therefore fail to encourage the indispensable growth of a community conscience.

May these risks be far from you and may the relationship of trust that binds you to the populace instead be ever closer, for it is in their service that you must operate with competence and a high sense of duty. Your mission as public administrators requires this of you; the Christian faith upon which many of you model your lives also demands it of you.

SPEECH TO THE BASILICATA REGION'S POLITICIANS AND ADMINISTRATORS, POTENZA, ITALY
April 28, 1991

You showed yourself to be Mother:
Mother of the Church, missionary on the paths of the Earth toward the coming third Christian Millennium;
Mother of men, through the constant protection that has warded off irreparable destructions and disasters and encouraged progress and modern social victories;.
Mother of nations, through the unlooked-for changes that have restored faith to peoples too long oppressed and humiliated;
Mother of life, through the many signs with which you have accompanied us, defending us from evil and from the power of death;
Mother to me for my whole life, and especially on that thirteenth of May 1981, when I felt at my side your succoring presence;
Mother of all men, who fights on behalf of the life that does not die;
Mother of mankind redeemed by the blood of Christ;
Mother of perfect love, of hope and of peace, Holy Mother of the Redeemer.

The motherly vigil of Mary, what an inscrutable experience! What a message, engraved mysteriously in a woman's heart, a woman who lived exclusively for God! Truly: "The Mighty One has done great things for her, and holy is his name" (cf. Lk 1:49).

There remain in our awareness at least these two moments: the night of Bethlehem and the "night of the Spirit" beneath her Son's Cross on Golgotha. And one other moment: the supper in Jerusalem on the day of Pentecost, when the Church came into existence, when the Church came into the world, like a newborn baby issuing from its mother's womb.

The Church brought with it this motherly watchfulness of Mary, giving expression to it in so many sanctuaries around the world. It lives every day through the gift of this maternal concern. Here, on this Earth, in this country in which we are meeting, the generations live with the knowledge that the Mother watches over them. From here, from Jasna Góra, she watches over all the people, over every one. Especially in the most difficult moments, amid trials and dangers.

PRAYER VIGIL, WORLD YOUTH DAY VI, CZĘSTOCHOWA, POLAND
August 14, 1991

We sometimes hear people criticizing the younger generations for seeking an easier life, for being hesitant to make lasting commitments and for taking life with a certain superficiality. Everyone, however, acknowledges that young people have a profound aspiration for liberty and an authenticity of relationships, a desire for more genuine justice and a brighter future for every human being. Dear young men and women, you are being asked to grow in responsibility and maturity, taking on all commitments with consistency and courage. This is especially necessary in the times in which we are now living, as we experience radical and sometimes challenging social changes. Shadows and difficulties, of course, are present, but you are not the ones to allow yourselves to be intimidated. Shout to the world that Christ lives. Have the courage of Christian liberty! The Gospel is demanding, it is true, but it is worth the trouble of following it, because it carries within itself the secret of the full satisfaction of all the heart's most noble aspirations.

SPEECH TO YOUTH, VICENZA, ITALY
September 8, 1991

I would like to thank you children for your presence, and for your noise. I thank you for this noise, because this noise is a sign of hope for the world. And I would like to add that today is a feast day, a feast very close to all you children: today the Church is celebrating the Nativity of the Virgin Mary. And I believe that even this little creature, this tiny newborn girl, must certainly have made noise. But what hope that noise represented for all of mankind! So I thank you for this noise, the noise of children, the noise of little ones. Jesus loved you for it, and did not wish to be rid of this noise. The apostles wished to rid him of the noise, they would not let the mothers come and bring their children to him. Instead, he said, "Let the children come to me. Let the children come." And then he said something very interesting: "For the kingdom of heaven belongs to such as these" (Mt 19:14). That is why the noise of the little ones, of children, is so precious. It is so precious because it speaks to us of the kingdom of God, this kingdom that is the future, the future destiny of mankind. This kingdom is in you. You carry it in your hearts. These hearts are pure. These hearts are sincere. These hearts are full of love.

SPEECH TO FIRST COMMUNION CHILDREN AND CONFIRMATION CLASS, VICENZA, ITALY
September 8, 1991

What is beautiful in you is that you all look after each other and take one
another by the hand without regard to color, social condition, or religion. You
take one another by the hand. If only grown-ups could be like you and stop all
their discrimination. That is the only way that the world can achieve peace. If
it is so important to be children, then all children are important. All children
are important, all of them. There cannot and must not be abandoned children.
Nor children without families. Nor street children. There cannot and must
not be children used by adults for immoral purposes, for drug trafficking, for
petty or major crimes, for the practice of vice. There cannot and must not be
children in reform schools and in houses of correction, where it is impossible
for them to obtain a genuine education. There cannot and must not be – this
is the Pope who asks this and demands it in the name of God and of his Son,
who was a child himself, Jesus – there cannot and must not be children killed,
murdered on the pretext of preventing crimes, targeted for death.

SPEECH TO CHILDREN, SALVADOR, BRAZIL
October 20, 1991

"Blessed are you, Mary, among women!" In the train of this greeting from Elizabeth, we too would now like to lift a canticle of praise to the Virgin: "Blessed are you among women, and blessed is the fruit of your womb." Blessed are you, O Mary, model of our faith and living image of our journey toward Christ. Blessed are you, Virgin Mary, model of charity and motherly love for all those in search of consolation. Blessed are you, who engendered for us the source of life. Blessed because you associated each of us to the redeeming suffering of Christ Crucified, and you summoned us to serve those who suffer. Blessed are you, because you lead us on the path of the Gospel, and you urge us to do what he, your Son, will tell us to do along the roads of the world. Blessed are you, because you teach us to love the poor, the humble, the sinners, as God loves them.

HOLY MASS FOR THE ROMAN ORGANIZATION FOR PILGRIMAGES AND UNITALSI (NATIONAL ITALIAN UNION FOR TRANSPORTING THE SICK TO LOURDES AND INTERNATIONAL SHRINES)
February 11, 1992

These generations of slaves make me reflect that Jesus Christ chose to become a slave, who became a servant. He brought the light of the revelation of God into slavery. The revelation of God that means "God-love." Here you see injustice everywhere. It is a tragedy of a civilization that claimed to be Christian. The great ancient philosopher Socrates said that those who suffer injustice are in a better position than those who cause it. This is the other side of the reality of the injustice that was experienced in this place. It is a human tragedy: the cries of generations demand that we free ourselves for all time of this tragedy, because its roots are in us, in human nature, in sin. I have come to pay tribute to all the unknown victims. Unfortunately, our civilization that claimed and still claims to be Christian, returned briefly, even during this century, to the practice of slavery. We know what the death camps were. Here is an early model. We cannot immerse ourselves in the tragedy of our civilization and of our weakness. We must remain faithful to another cry, that of Saint Paul who told us: "Ubi abundavit peccatum, superabundavit gratia" (Rom 5:20)— "Where sin increased, grace overflowed all the more."

VISIT TO THE HOUSE OF SLAVES, ISLAND OF GORÉE, SENEGAL
February 22, 1992

What better wish and commitment, beloved young people, than to set out to rediscover and encounter the presence of Jesus Christ, source of life, of the full life?

Jesus Christ! He alone fully answers our aspiration for truth, beauty, and happiness.

In the midst of great historical shifts, in the face of epochal collapses and grave and enduring concerns, there is so much need for your emerging strength, need for your capacity to build — on that cornerstone — new forms of life that are more worthy of man.

ANGELUS, WORLD YOUTH DAY VII, SAINT PETER'S SQUARE, VATICAN CITY
April 12, 1992

And so the Cross of Christ has remained in the history of man as the sign of love that removes sin. It is good that at the end of this day we are all present here, in the ancient Roman Colosseum, at the center of a city that has experienced the saga of the martyrs. Here, in the Rome of the Caesars, man came to understand, in a particularly profound manner, the mystery of the Cross. Those who gave their lives for Christ at the dawn of Christianity do not cease from testifying to the power of the Cross. They have each in their own flesh completed "what was lacking in the afflictions of Christ on behalf of his Body, which is the Church" (Col 1:24).

The ruins of the Colosseum do not cease from speaking of this! And behold, it opens out like an immense space that only God can penetrate. In this space are present all those who, in different ways, participate in the sufferings of Christ. They look to the Cross, perhaps not even knowing that they are embraced by the very mystery of redemptive love, which knows no limits.

SPEECH AT THE END OF THE WAY OF THE CROSS AT THE COLOSSEUM, ROME, ITALY
April 17, 1992

Mary is young in her motherhood. As a mother, she gives freely what she has freely received. She does not close herself up, she does not try to keep to herself the gift that the All Highest has bestowed upon her, but readily takes it to others and conceives the Son of God incarnate in order to redeem all of mankind. This freeness, made up of readiness, attention, tenderness, and concrete actions, is the other face of Mary's youth. By looking at her, we learn that youth belongs to those who always know how to offer new love, those who never wait for others to take the initiative, but know instead how to be first in love. Mary is young in this way: so overbrimming with the free gift of the Father that she becomes transparency itself and communicates in turn to her brothers. In great haste, in fact, she hurries to her elderly cousin and "when Elizabeth heard Mary's greeting, the infant leaped in her womb" (Lk 1:41). Guided by radiant love, Mary knew how to understand Elizabeth's need and to be there for her with generosity and solicitude. She thus teaches us that youth is generosity, attention to others, the capacity to approach them and to serve them substantially, faithfully, and humbly in simple acts.

MEETING WITH YOUTH, SANTA MARIA CAPUA VETERE, ITALY
May 24, 1992

My brothers and friends, reject decisively, with your word and your example, the deceptive propaganda in favor of abortion; reject the criminal annihilation of innocent, defenseless persons. Young people who are preparing for life, always respect motherhood! The defense of life extends for the full duration of life itself, from the moment of conception until its natural end. Thus education is also the defense of life, and the nuclear family must serve as a faithful transmitter of human values and Christian faith. Christian parents, take seriously your obligation to provide a humane and Christian education to your children. They are your continuance. Give them the best that you have: a clear conscience, a Christian life, the capacity to be useful and well-prepared members of society and of the country. Lift your gaze to the Holy Family of Nazareth! Look at the hidden way of life that the Son of God led with Mary and Joseph.

Dear friends, love is not only a spontaneous or instinctive thing: it is a decision to be confirmed constantly. When a man and a woman are joined by true love, they each take to themselves the destiny, the future of the other as their own, at the cost of hard work and sufferings, so that the other "may have life, and have it more abundantly" (Jn 10:10). These words of Jesus refer to all true love. It is only thus that people love seriously, and not as a game or for just a fleeting moment. Hearing the words "I love you," the other person will understand that these words are true and will also take seriously the experience of love. You must love as Jesus does. The most profound reason for Christian love is found in the words and the example of Christ: "Love one another as I love you" (Jn 15:12). This is true for every category of human love, it is true for the love of engaged couples, the love that is in preparation for marriage and family.

MEETING WITH LOMBARD YOUTH, CARAVAGGIO, ITALY
June 20, 1992

187

And love that is leading to marriage is also preparing for the creation of new life. This task should be considered a gift from God and a great act of faith toward other human beings. In this vision of things, children are nothing to be afraid of, they are not there to "steal" anyone's freedom, they are not intruders who take away our time, energy, and money. Children are not unwanted guests, but rather blessings from a god who shatters all selfishness in a couple and helps us to live life with gratitude and liberating love.

MEETING WITH LOMBARD YOUTH, CARAVAGGIO, ITALY
June 20, 1992

Man belongs to God inasmuch as he is made in his image; created in the image and semblance of God. Man, then, belongs to God in a different manner than all other visible creatures. He it is who climbs the mountain of the Lord. He is called, in the very depths of his spiritual being, to search for God: to search for his face. He is summoned to stand in the holy place of his Lord on account of the very profundity of his divine image and semblance. Man enters into a dynamic and vital process through which he matures, passing through innocent hands and a pure heart, attaining victory over sin and over anyone who lies and defames his neighbor. In this way, man belongs to God. Among all creatures, he is the recipient of a particular benediction of the Creator.

HOLY MASS FOR THE DEAD, CAMPO VERANO CEMETERY, ROME, ITALY
November 1, 1992

Since I must learn something from you, I thought I would ask what you call this thing you are holding in your hands: pom-pom. But I'd like to ask you something more: What do you have in your hearts? In your hands you have pom-poms, and in your hearts? There are a number of different answers, but I can't hear what you have. Jesus! All right, then, we shouldn't say what do you have, but who do you have in your heart. You have Jesus because Jesus says, "I am with you"; in fact, he says more than that. He says that he has come to live in us, with his Father. And for me it is a joy that you have Jesus in your hearts, because I have come here into your community, into your parish, I've come in the name of Jesus and to perform his mission. I see you all gathered here together – children, young men and women, your parents, the nuns who teach you, your priests. I see you all gathered around Jesus because he unites us, he makes us part of his community. This community of his, of Jesus's, where he is at the center, what is it called? The Church! Good, I see that the little ones have great wisdom, wisdom of the heart and also wisdom of the intellect. I am very happy with this meeting, with your answers, with what you have taught me and what I have learned. Now I will remember clearly that this is called a pom-pom.

VISIT TO THE PARISH OF SAINT MARY IMMACULATE OF LOURDES, ROME, ITALY
November 8, 1992

You must hear the cries of pain and sorrow of millions of people in the presence of the scandal caused by the "paradox of abundance" that constitutes the principal obstacle to the solution of the problem of nutrition for mankind. World food production — as you know very well — is sufficiently abundant to fully satisfy the needs of even a growing population, provided that the resources necessary for adequate nutrition were shared in accordance with real needs. I cannot but agree with the words that open your draft World Declaration on Nutrition: "Hunger and malnutrition are *unacceptable* in a *world* that has both the knowledge and the *resources* to end this human *catastrophe.*" Yet this paradox continues to cause tragic consequences every day.

SPEECH TO THE WORLD CONFERENCE ON NUTRITION, ROME, ITALY
December 5, 1992

The greatest Friend! Yes, dear friends, Jesus really is the greatest Friend that God could give to children. He is the big brother who gave his life for us. He called us friends (Jn 15:14) and he considers us all and always to be his friends, but especially the little ones. Not only did he say, "Let the children come to me, and do not prevent them; for the kingdom of heaven belongs to such as these" (Mt 19:14), but he also added: "Whoever receives one child such as this in my name receives me" (Mt 18:5). Jesus, therefore, should be considered by young people as a friend. He himself said what that entails: "You are my friends if you do what I command you" (Jn 15:14). We are friends of Jesus if we listen to and put into practice his words.

Beloved brothers and sisters! The ceremony of baptism, rich in symbolism, biblical references, and significant acts, encourages us to reflect on the mystery of all human destiny. To be born means entering into a specific divine plan: no one comes into the world by chance; everyone, in fact, has a particular mission to perform, which of course we cannot know fully from the start, but which one day will be completely revealed. Let us be guided, then, by the awareness that we are instruments of God, who created us out of love and who wishes to be repaid in our love. This is the wish, charged with hope, that I express wholeheartedly to these children and to all you who accompany them. May each of you always perform the mission that God has entrusted to you, even among the vicissitudes and the difficulties of human life.

BAPTISM OF THIRTY-NINE CHILDREN
January 2, 1993

The world needs peace, harmony, and mutual understanding. The divine Master bequeathed to the Church and to the men of all times his perennial testament of love: "Love one another as I love you!" (Jn 15:12). A sense of great sadness floods the heart when we think of the infinite goodness of God and the human indifference, the hatred, and the wars that cloud the plan of divine Providence on Earth. You, with your prayer and with the testimony of goodness, can offer a daily contribution to the cause of the pacification of hearts and the establishment of peace among men. I have come to tell you that the Pope relies on your hidden but effective contribution: ask God for the gift of peace to hearts, to families, and to peoples. Beloved ones! In the face of the tragedies of men, prayers may seem ineffective and vain, but they always open new glimpses of hope, especially when they are enhanced by the pain that is transformed into love.

When I walked among you here and when I greeted you, an expression in English came into my mind: "to shake hands." It is a thing that we do so often. I too have done this with many of you and before that with other people. It is a customary thing, a routine thing, a tradition, but it also has a certain significance. When we shake hands with other people, it means that we are close to them, that we know one another; in fact, that we wish to live in a certain "alliance," a friendship. In Italian the phrase is *dare la mano*, which also means to lend a hand, to offer help. So you see that this simple gesture, so ordinary and routine, has many meanings!

VISIT TO THE PARISH OF SAINT HELENA, ROME, ITALY
January 17, 1993

Your friend said that the Pope is good. But I don't think that he is good at all, because he was not able to greet everyone that is here, all of you . . . but most of you, at least. I also greet all the others through those that I have been able to embrace. Do you know what thirst is? Have any of you, any boys or any girls, ever been thirsty? When you are thirsty, you seek water. And, in fact, Jesus was thirsty in Samaria, near a well. And the Lord was also thirsty on the Cross: "I am thirsty." But Jesus, as today's Liturgy reminds us, met a Samaritan woman near this well, and he said to her, "Give me a drink" (Jn 4:7). And Jesus said to her what he expressed elsewhere, "Let anyone who thirsts come to me and drink" (Jn 7:37). On the one hand, there is physical thirst, when you need water; on the other hand, those who have thirst should come to Jesus and drink. Because he too is a well. But here we are talking about a spiritual thirst, not a physical thirst. Physical thirst, when our body needs to drink, can be sated by water. But there is also a thirst of the spirit, of our soul; and this thirst cannot be quenched, cannot be sated, except through Jesus.

VISIT TO THE PARISH OF THE MOST HOLY SACRAMENT, ROME, ITALY
March 14, 1993

Faith — just like your fields of grain, your fruit orchards, your olive groves — needs to be cultivated. It is not enough that you have received it, nor is it sufficient to preserve it like a precious object, hidden in a coffer. In the first Letter to the Corinthians, Saint Paul mentions a field in which his preaching is sown and irrigated, so that God can then make it grow. In the end, he concludes: "You are God's field!" (3:9). No one more than you, tillers of the soil, can grasp the appropriateness and profundity of that comparison. You have the good fortune — so rare nowadays, especially for those who live in the deafening noise of the cities — to touch directly every day the miracle of nature. You are given the opportunity to sense, in the budding of new life, the perennial mystery of Creation. If this is true for nature, how much more true it is on the supernatural plane! In the field of human hearts, the miracle of faith is the work of grace, a gift of God. All is grace!

SPEECH TO FARMERS, VESCOVÌO DI TORRI, ITALY
March 19, 1993

The adoration of the Cross endures over the centuries, in the succession of generations. Our century too—this twentieth century—has experienced the bitter reality of religious persecution in the modern colosseums of Europe and the world, both East and West. Centuries later, there are still people who, just like the Christians in pagan ancient Rome, are willing to adore the Cross with the sacrifice of their own lives, who are willing to embrace the Cross with the supreme testimony of martyrdom, Christians who went to their deaths crying: *Ave Crux!* Their death, thanks to the Cross of Christ, becomes the seed of a new life.

SPEECH AT THE END OF THE WAY OF THE CROSS AT THE COLOSSEUM, ROME, ITALY
April 9, 1993

When man opens his heart to faith, he experiences the replacement of selfishness by altruism, hatred by love, revenge by forgiveness, greed by loving service, egoism and individualism by solidarity, division by concord – just like the name of the ancient temple near Agrigento – and violence by mercy. This happens when man opens his heart to faith. When, instead, he rejects the Gospel and its message of salvation, it begins a process of erosion of moral values, which is likely to have negative repercussions on the larger life of society. The true force capable of defeating these destructive tendencies springs from faith. This, however, demands not only an intimate personal decision, but also a courageous external testimony, which expresses itself in a firm condemnation of evil. This demands, here, in your land, a clear rejection of the culture of the Mafia, which is a culture of death, profoundly inhuman, anti-evangelical, and inimical to individual dignity and civil coexistence.

HOLY MASS, AGRIGENTO, ITALY
May 9, 1993

In the modern era, humanity has achieved extraordinary scientific and technological progress, while at the same time often losing track of the true answers to the great questions of life. And that is tragic. All around is a sense of insecurity that clips the wings of commitment, undermines enthusiasm, leads us to solutions of compromise or even of surrender. How can we be authentic Christians in a world where so little is Christian? How can we live our faith in an environment that is hostile to it or, at the very least, dismisses it with patronizing indifference? That is what the world is like.

Beloved young people, it is not easy to be Christian these days, we must recognize that. It is necessary to swim against the stream. Faith is no longer taken for granted, as it might have been in other times. It is a decision in which each of us is required to invest himself with his personal convictions, defying the surrounding environment.

Faith, beloved young people, is like gold: it is purified in the fire. In order to be authentic, it must pass through the Cross of Christ.

MEETING WITH YOUTH, AREZZO, ITALY
May 23, 1993

In the month of May, the Church prays with special intensity to Mary, Mother of God, entrusting to her the lives of men and peoples in today's world. To her who is our Mother and the Queen of Peace we entrust in a special manner the peace of the world, but especially in Europe, in the Balkans. Through her we turn to Christ, Redeemer of the world, summoning to mind the words with which we prayed at the beginning of this year, during the meeting in Assisi: "O Lord, knock down the barriers of hatred that divide the nations. . . . There where sin now abounds, make justice and love overflow, the justice and love to which every man, every people, and every nation is summoned in You."

PRAYER TO OUR LADY OF LOURDES, VATICAN GARDENS
May 31, 1993

The Eucharist of which you will become ministers is not a rite separate from life. The priest, on the altar, joins the faithful to the sacrifice of Christ, offering not only their prayers, but also all their good works, their joys and their sorrows, their pleas and their praises, thus ensuring that the lives of the faithful are an offering to God. In your priestly hands, dear brothers, Christ will deposit the immense treasure of redemption, of the remission of sins. I want to exhort you to ensure that in the ministry that you are undertaking here today, you do not overlook the sacrament of reconciliation, in which all Christians receive forgiveness for their sins. Encourage a pastoral activity that will lead the faithful to personal conversion, and in order to do so, you must dedicate to your ministry all the time necessary, with the generosity and patience of authentic fishers of men.

HOLY MASS FOR THE ORDINATION OF THIRTY-FIVE NEW PRIESTS, SEVILLE, SPAIN
June 12, 1993

The relationship between man's freedom and God's law is most deeply lived out in the "heart" of the person, in his moral conscience. As the Second Vatican Council observed: "In the depths of his conscience man detects a law which he does not impose on himself, but which holds him to obedience. Always summoning him to love good and avoid evil, the voice of conscience can when necessary speak to his heart more specifically: 'do this, shun that.' For man has in his heart a law written by God. To obey it is the very dignity of man; according to it he will be judged" (cf. Rom 2:14–16).

ENCYCLICAL VERITATIS SPLENDOR, § 54
August 6, 1993

I am already accustomed to being asked questions: young people subject me to an examination, and have done so for many years now. But I do my best to get through it, to overcome my difficulties, because young people are good. They encourage me, for instance, when they cry: "Long live the Pope." Which means: you must live, you must be strong. And I must obey.

Try always to be young! But there is one point in which you should not follow the young man in the Gospel, because he became sad after hearing the proposals of Jesus. He was sad because he felt incapable of giving a positive answer, of following him. I hope for you that you will never be sad, that you will always be joyful! That means following Jesus and doing whatever he asks of you. Follow him in your choice of vocation, follow Jesus. Follow him especially in the development of charity, the love of God and of your neighbor.

MEETING WITH YOUTH, ASTI, ITALY
September 26, 1993

Among these many paths, the family is the first and the most important.
It is a path common to all, yet one that is particular, unique, and unrepeatable,
just as every individual is unrepeatable; it is a path from which man cannot
withdraw. Indeed, a person normally comes into the world within a family,
and can be said to owe to the family the very fact of his existing as an individual.
When he has no family, the person coming into the world develops an
anguished sense of pain and loss, one that will subsequently burden his
whole life. The Church draws near with loving concern to all who experience
situations such as these, for she knows well the fundamental role that the
family is called upon to play. Furthermore, she knows that a person goes forth
from the family in order to realize in a new family unit his particular vocation
in life. Even if someone chooses to remain single, the family continues to be,
as it were, his existential horizon, that fundamental community in which
the whole network of social relations is grounded, from the closest and most
immediate to the most distant. Do we not often speak of the "human family"
when referring to all the people living in the world?

LETTER TO FAMILIES GRATISSIMAM SANE, § 2
February 2, 1994

The family has its origin in that same love with which the Creator embraces the created world, as was already expressed "in the beginning," in the book of Genesis (1:1). In the Gospel Jesus offers a supreme confirmation: "God so loved the world that he gave his only Son" (Jn 3:16). The only-begotten Son, of one substance with the Father, "God from God and Light from Light," entered into human history through the family: "For by his incarnation the Son of God united himself in a certain way with every man. He labored with human hands . . . and loved with a human heart. Born of Mary the Virgin, he truly became one of us and, except for sin, was like us in every respect." If, in fact, Christ "fully discloses man to himself," he does so beginning with the family in which he chose to be born and to grow up. We know that the Redeemer spent most of his life in the obscurity of Nazareth, "obedient" (Lk 2:51) as the "Son of Man" to Mary his Mother and to Joseph the carpenter. Is this filial "obedience" of Christ not already the first expression of that obedience to the Father "to death" (Phil 2:8), whereby he redeemed the world?

LETTER TO FAMILIES GRATISSIMAM SANE, § 2
February 2, 1994

Prayer makes the Son of God present among us: "For where two or three are gathered in my name, I am there among them" (Mt 18:20). Prayer must become the dominant element of the Year of the Family in the Church: prayer by the family, prayer for the family, and prayer with the family.

It is significant that precisely in and through prayer, man comes to discover in a very simple and yet profound way his own unique subjectivity: in prayer the human "I" more easily perceives the depth of what it means to be a person. This is also true of the family, which is not only the basic "cell" of society, but also possesses a particular subjectivity of its own. This subjectivity finds its first and fundamental confirmation, and is strengthened, precisely when the members of the family meet in the common invocation "our Father."

LETTER TO FAMILIES GRATISSIMAM SANE, § 4
February 2, 1994

The universe, immense and diverse as it is, the world of all living beings, is inscribed in God's fatherhood, which is its source. This can be said, of course, on the basis of an analogy, thanks to which we can discern, at the very beginning of the book of Genesis, the reality of fatherhood and motherhood and consequently of the human family. The interpretative key enabling this discernment is provided by the principle of the "image" and "likeness" of God highlighted by the scriptural text. God creates by the power of his word: "Let there be . . . !" Significantly, in the Creation of man this word of God is followed by these other words: "Let us make man in our image, after our likeness." Before creating man, the Creator withdraws as it were into himself, in order to seek the pattern and inspiration in the mystery of his Being, which is already here disclosed as the divine "We." From this mystery the human being comes forth by an act of Creation: "God created man in his own image, in the image of God he created him; male and female he created them" (Gn 1:27).

LETTER TO FAMILIES GRATISSIMAM SANE, § 6
February 2, 1994

It is for themselves that married couples want children; in children they see the crowning of their own love for each other. They want children for the family, as a priceless gift. This is quite understandable. Nonetheless, in conjugal love and in paternal and maternal love we should find inscribed the same truth about man that the Council expressed in a clear and concise way in its statement that God "willed man for his own sake." It is thus necessary that the will of the parents should be in harmony with the will of God. They must want the new human creature in the same way as the Creator wants him: "for himself." Our human will is always and inevitably subject to the law of time and change. The divine will, on the other hand, is eternal. . . . "Before I formed you in the womb I knew you, and before you were born I consecrated you" (Jer 1:5).

LETTER TO FAMILIES GRATISSIMAM SANE, § 9
February 2, 1994

Dearest ones, today I wish for you this strong faith. The faith of children and young people is always strong and ardent, it expresses itself with prayer, with the love of Jesus. And so it is easy to understand that someone like you could give their life to Jesus. I wish that for you today, on this clean, fresh springlike Sunday. Everything speaks of youth, everything is rejuvenating.

Nature is rejuvenating, flowers are budding. This rejuvenation of nature also speaks of the youth in human nature, in us.

So I ask, with the young people, here: what should we pray for? I think that perhaps we should pray for money. Yes, for money, to have the resources to reach the next leg of the trip, Manila, in the Philippines. Travel is expensive.

Certainly, young people need money for many things: to live, to develop, to get an education, to prepare for adult life, to live honestly. Because we do not want money that is other than honest. Absolutely not. We want to get money in an honest way and spend that money in an honest way as well. As we demonstrated in Denver, for that matter, because many things were predicted and expected of us: people predicted and thought that young people might be thieves or violent. But we had a surprise in store for our American friends. They had prepared with vast forces, with substantial economic means. But the young people did none of the things that were feared: they didn't steal, they weren't violent; none of that; they won through honesty.

I rejoice with you, young people, who wish to remain in the presence of the Eucharist, because in the "poor" sign of the bread and the wine you recognize the presence of Christ, the Way, the Truth, and the Life. You know how to listen to the words of Jesus as if they were addressed personally to each one of you: "Take and eat; this is my body. . . . Drink from it, all of you" (Mt 26:26–27). They render newly present an event in which the supernatural vocation of every man is indicated: to be a gift and to make oneself a gift. I rejoice with you, young Italians, who fix the gaze of your soul on Jesus in the Eucharist, a gift of the Father: you can thus discover your call as a project to be implemented day after day, in freedom and in dedication.

SPEECH TO YOUTH, SIENA, ITALY
June 4, 1994

To forgive means freeing the heart of sentiments of revenge, feelings that would not be in keeping with the civilization of love to which all people of goodwill are committed to offer their own contribution. Peace implies that underlying every initiative there always be a sincere willingness to engage in dialogue, a respect for the rights of everyone, including national minorities, and a commitment to reciprocal tolerance. May you always have the clear certainty that the good of peace has its ultimate foundation in the very heart of God.

FAREWELL SPEECH, ZAGREB INTERNATIONAL AIRPORT, CROATIA
September 11, 1994

Youth is this period of human life where you plan out the rest of your life. A young person begins to plan out his life and he lives with this plan and tries to carry it out, to prepare himself to carry it out. In other words, this is also called a vocation, because the plan that you, dear girl, dear boy, find to be your own property comes at the same time from God, it is suggested by the Holy Spirit, and it requires a collaboration with the Holy Spirit to identify this plan, explore it more deeply, and then to carry it out properly; to find happiness, because a completed plan brings this happiness with it, this happiness to which God calls us. We are all called to happiness in God, through this plan of ours that also comes from him. It is accepted by us, it is carried out by us, and then it finds its final step in God himself.

SPEECH TO YOUTH, LECCE, ITALY
September 18, 1994

Now let us think: Did Jesus ever make his Mother Mary cry? When he was a child like you, when he was a youngster like you, did he ever make his Mother cry? Certainly not. We know that on one occasion he did cause her and Saint Joseph a certain amount of concern, when he was twelve and he remained in the Temple of Jerusalem. But there was a reason for that: he had to emphasize the mission that his Heavenly Father had assigned to him in the service of all mankind. Then, however, he went back with his parents to their house in Nazareth and he was always obedient, full of goodness and wisdom.

I would like to tell all of you: Don't ever make your parents unhappy! Don't ever make your mother and father cry. You can only make them cry tears of joy when you behave well, and that is a lovely thing. Certainly the Madonna too was overjoyed and moved when she saw Jesus praying, helping out around the house and in the workshop, being good, being a friend to all. . . . Well, I wish for you these tears of joy shed by your parents at how well you behave yourselves.

SPEECH TO CHILDREN, SIRACUSA, SICILY
November 6, 1994

In Jesus Christ, God not only speaks to man but also seeks him out. The Incarnation of the Son of God attests that God goes in search of man. Jesus speaks of this search as the finding of a lost sheep (cf. Lk 15:1–7). It is a search that begins in the heart of God and culminates in the Incarnation of the Word. If God goes in search of man, created in his own image and likeness, he does so because he loves him eternally in the Word and wishes to raise him in Christ to the dignity of an adoptive son. God therefore goes in search of man who is his special possession in a way unlike any other creature. Man is God's possession by virtue of a choice made in love: God seeks man out, moved by his fatherly heart.

APOSTOLIC LETTER TERTIO MILLENNIO ADVENIENTE, § 7
November 10, 1994

Earlier I was speaking to you about the "Gospel of children": has this not found in our own time a particular expression in the spirituality of Saint Theresa of the Child Jesus? It is absolutely true: Jesus and his Mother often choose children and give them important tasks for the life of the Church and of humanity. I have named only a few who are known everywhere, but how many others there are who are less widely known! The Redeemer of humanity seems to share with them his concern for others: for parents, for other boys and girls. He eagerly awaits their prayers. What enormous power the prayer of children has! This becomes a model for grown-ups themselves: praying with simple and complete trust means praying as children pray.

217

Raise your tiny hand, Divine Child,
and bless these young friends of yours,
bless the children of all the Earth.

LETTER TO CHILDREN
December 13, 1994

You ask, what are my expectations of young people? In *Crossing the Threshold of Hope* I have written that "the fundamental problem of youth is profoundly personal. Young people . . . know that their life has meaning to the extent that it becomes a free gift for others" (p. 121). A question therefore is directed to each one of you personally: Are you capable of giving of yourself, your time, your energies, your talents, for the good of others? Are you capable of love? If you are, the Church and society can expect great things from each one of you.

WORLD YOUTH DAY X, MANILA, PHILIPPINES
January 14, 1995

On this banner is written: "Have no fear." But you do not have fear. It's clear, you are courageous. Indeed, you are ready to encourage the Pope. That is why I had to write to children, in part so that I could be encouraged by them: encouraged with their letters, with their presence, with their prayers, with the catechism in which they are participating. All this is the dialogue between the Pope and the children.

It is a good dialogue! I receive many letters in response, and not only from Rome, but from all over Italy and from other parts of the world. And so, I would like to continue along this road without fear and, in fact, also follow your advice: you said that the Pope must be ever better. This is right. We must all be ever better and the Pope, perhaps more than anyone else, must be ever better. I will try to do so!

I want to encourage you to be good boys and girls, good children—in your families, in your neighborhood, in the schools, in your parish—so that you can bring this joy to everyone. Just walking into this room, one immediately sees, one senses the joy. You bring joy to others, you are our joy and you remain our joy. This is my wish for you.

VISIT TO THE PARISH OF SAINT JEANNE-ANTIDE THOURET, ROME, ITALY
March 12, 1995

O Mary, Mother of Jesus
And wife of Joseph the artisan,
In your heart are gathered
The joys and the hardships
Of the Holy Family.

Even the hours of pain and grief
You offered to God,
Always trusting
In his Providence.

Protect, we implore you,
All the women
Who work hard every day
So that the domestic community
Can live in productive harmony.

Let them become women
Of Christian wisdom,
Experts in prayer and humanity,
Strong in times of hope
And in tribulations,
Artisans, like you,
Of authentic peace. Amen.

ANGELUS, CAMPOBASSO, ITALY
March 19, 1995

Man is called to a fullness of life that far exceeds the dimensions of his earthly existence, because it consists in sharing the very life of God. The loftiness of this supernatural vocation reveals the greatness and the inestimable value of human life even in its temporal phase. Life in time, in fact, is the fundamental condition, the initial stage and an integral part of the entire unified process of human existence. It is a process that, unexpectedly and undeservedly, is enlightened by the promise and renewed by the gift of divine life, which will reach its full realization in eternity (cf. 1 Jn 3:1–2). At the same time, it is precisely this supernatural calling that highlights the relative character of each individual's earthly life. After all, life on Earth is not an "ultimate" but a "penultimate" reality; even so, it remains a sacred reality entrusted to us, to be preserved with a sense of responsibility and brought to perfection in love and in the gift of ourselves to God and to our brothers and sisters.

ENCYCLICAL EVANGELIUM VITAE, § 2
March 25, 1995

Life is always a good. This is an instinctive perception and a fact of experience, and man is called to grasp the profound reason why this is so.

"Let us make man in our image, after our likeness" (Gn 1:26). The life that God offers to man is a gift by which God shares something of himself with his creature.

ENCYCLICAL EVANGELIUM VITAE, § 34
March 25, 1995

"What are humans that you are mindful of them, mere mortals that you care for them?" the Psalmist wonders (Ps 8:4). Compared to the immensity of the universe, man is very small, and yet this very contrast reveals his greatness: "You have made them little less than a god, and crowned them with glory and honor" (Ps 8:5). The glory of God shines on the face of man. In man the Creator finds his rest, as Saint Ambrose comments with a sense of awe: "The sixth day is finished and the Creation of the world ends with the formation of that masterpiece that is man, who exercises dominion over all living creatures and is as it were the crown of the universe and the supreme beauty of every created being. Truly we should maintain a reverential silence, since the Lord rested from every work he had undertaken in the world. He rested then in the depths of man, he rested in man's mind and in his thought; after all, he had created man endowed with reason, capable of imitating him, of emulating his virtue, of hungering for heavenly graces" (*Hexameron* VI.75–76).

ENCYCLICAL EVANGELIUM VITAE, § 35
March 25, 1995

This is the model against which we should strive to shape ourselves! The Trinity, beloved young people, teaches you first and foremost that everyone must try to be themselves. An adolescent, a young person, is someone who is still shaping his own identity. In this society of consumption and image in which we live, we run the risk of easily losing ourselves, of winding up shattered into fragments. A mirror in fragments can no longer reflect a whole image. It must be reconstructed. A person therefore needs a profound and stable center, around which he can unify his various experiences. This center, as Saint Augustine teaches us, cannot be sought outside ourselves, but only in our own heart, where the man meets God the Father, the Son, and the Holy Spirit. It is in the relationship with God who is unity that man can unify himself.

I offer thanks to God for being born and for having been called to this particular mission of mine. I want to thank him for the gift of the sacrament of the priesthood and of the episcopate, and I pray incessantly to the Holy Spirit to help me to remain faithful to them until the day I die.

I offer thanks to God because my life and my priestly, episcopal, and pontifical ministry fall in a moment of momentous change for Europe, for the world, and for the Church. How can I not be thankful for the twenty years of episcopal ministry in my beloved church of Cracow? How can I fail to express my gratitude for the gift of participation in the Second Vatican Council, which pointed the paths of the Church toward the third Christian millennium? How can I fail to remember today, with trepidation in my heart, the date of October 16, 1978, when, through the call of the Conclave, I heard the summons of Christ: "Feed my lambs!" (Jn 21:15)?

SPEECH ON HIS SEVENTY-FIFTH BIRTHDAY
May 17, 1995

I know that among you there are young Christians of various confessions, young people of other religions, and also young people in search of God. I am happy for this brotherly meeting: it is important for young people, who may well belong to different cultures and traditions, to form a great pilgrimage along the roads of the world, a pilgrimage of peace and reconciliation.

Dear friends, spread the truth with love. Resist the appeal of those who push you to affirm alleged truths or values with violence or falsehood. The truth affirms itself on its own, with the force that is inherent to it. You too, dear friends, become witnesses to the truth in love.

VIDEO MESSAGE TO GENFEST '95
May 20, 1995

Prayer, the community at prayer, enables us always to discover anew the evangelical truth of the words: "You have but one Father" (Mt 23:9), the Father—Abba—invoked by Christ himself, the Only-Begotten and Consubstantial Son. And again: "You have but one teacher, and you are all brothers" (Mt 23:8). "Ecumenical" prayer discloses this fundamental dimension of brotherhood in Christ, who died to gather together the children of God who were scattered, so that in becoming "sons and daughters in the Son," we might show forth more fully both the mysterious reality of God's fatherhood and the truth about the human nature shared by each and every individual.

ENCYCLICAL UT UNUM SINT, § 26
May 25, 1995

God is love and in him there is not a shadow of evil. Then whence comes the violence that so frequently devastates human history? A believer knows the answer: it comes from the wrong use of that wonderful gift that is liberty; it comes from the human selfishness that accommodates the lying overtures of the devil, enemy of God and of man. God wants humanity to form an ever greater single family, but an enemy sows discord in order to engender enmity between man and God and between man and man. Christ Jesus, with his Death and Resurrection, freed us from the power of sin. He is our Paschal Lamb and our Peace!

I invite you always to serve your country in a universal spirit of openness and solidarity toward everyone, without bias or discrimination. In traveling the world's oceans from one country to another, be builders of peace among peoples. Peace flows from justice, and justice is dependent on truth, the truth concerning God and concerning the meaning and purpose of human life, for we have been created in the image and likeness of God himself.

SPEECH TO THE CADETS OF THE STATE UNIVERSITY OF NEW YORK MARITIME COLLEGE
June 19, 1995

The respect for full equality between men and women in every walk of life is a great triumph of civilization. Women contributed to it with their painful and generous daily testifying, but also with the organized movements that, especially in our century, have placed this topic at the focus of universal attention. Equality between men and women is, in fact, stated from the very first page of the Bible, in the magnificent account of Creation. The book of Genesis says, "God created man in his image, in the divine image he created him; male and female he created them" (Gn 1:27). In these concise lines there emerges the profound reason for the greatness of man: he carries stamped within himself the image of God! This is equally true for men and women, both marked by the imprint of the Creator.

ANGELUS
June 25, 1995

Thank you, women who are mothers! You have sheltered human beings within yourselves in a unique experience of joy and travail. This experience makes you become God's own smile upon the newborn child, the one who guides your child's first steps, who helps it to grow, and who is the anchor as the child makes its way along the journey of life.

Thank you, women who are wives! You irrevocably join your future to that of your husbands, in a relationship of mutual giving, at the service of love and life.

Thank you, women who are daughters and women who are sisters! Into the heart of the family, and then of all society, you bring the richness of your sensitivity, your intuitiveness, your generosity and fidelity.

LETTER TO WOMEN, § 2
June 29, 1995

Thank you, women who work! You are present and active in every area of life — social, economic, cultural, artistic, and political. In this way you make an indispensable contribution to the growth of a culture that unites reason and feeling, to a model of life ever open to the sense of "mystery," to the establishment of economic and political structures ever more worthy of humanity.

Thank you, consecrated women! Following the example of the greatest of women, the Mother of Jesus Christ, the Incarnate Word, you open yourselves with obedience and fidelity to the gift of God's love. You help the Church and all mankind to experience a "spousal" relationship to God, one that magnificently expresses the fellowship that God wishes to establish with his creatures.

Thank you, every woman, for the simple fact of being a woman! Through the insight that is so much a part of your womanhood you enrich the world's understanding and help to make human relations more honest and authentic.

LETTER TO WOMEN, § 2
June 29, 1995

While, tragically, war rages in various parts of the world and there are those, not all that far from us, who live in the illusion that they can build peace on the basis of abuse and the oppression of national and personal identities, this concert, the fruit of the harmonious and deeply motivated action of people and instruments that are vastly diverse, reminds us, in contrast, that peace is possible only when individuals, accepting the richness of others, commit themselves to offering the best they have to give and heeding their own call, in an attitude of patient and determined dialogue.

APPEAL FOR RECONCILIATION IN EUROPE
August 13, 1995

Don't forget your roots. The tree that wishes to grow and bear fruit must draw
nourishment with its roots from good soil. Young people of Europe, the Gospel
is the soil in which you must sink the roots of your future! In the Gospel,
Christ comes toward you. Discover and savor his friendship, invite him to be
your traveling companion at every hour of every day. He alone has words of
eternal life.

MEETING WITH YOUTH, LORETO, ITALY
September 9, 1995

It is clear to everyone that the defense of life is a commitment that pertains not only to the realm of private morality, but is also a social and political issue; indeed it calls into question the very existence of political society. Consequently, commitment to the defense of life cannot fail to have its repercussions, with peaceful, convinced community action, in the realm of lifestyle, culture, and legislation.

The triumph of truth and life already belong to the history of salvation: it is the responsibility of all the forces committed to the respect of human dignity to inscribe it in the history of humanity.

SPEECH TO THE WORLD CONGRESS OF PRO-LIFE MOVEMENTS
October 3, 1995

It was wonderful your singing for peace. It was wonderful for it was for peace. And it was wonderful that you did so in song, for we know a great man, Saint Augustine – do you know him? Not so much. . . . Saint Augustine was a great doctor of the Church, a great philosopher, a theologian, he said, "Qui cantat bis orat" – Singing is praying twice. So in singing for peace, you are praying twice for peace. But I should say that, not only twice, you are praying three times, for you pray singing, so twice, and you pray as children, and children have a special power over the heart of the Father. So this prayer for peace you sang was very nice and very fruitful. And it will be fruitful, I am convinced.

It pleased God, in his goodness and wisdom, to reveal himself and the mystery of his will. A great mystery, this! A mystery that never ceases to arouse in the children of the Church worshipful astonishment. God, the perennial yearning of the human heart, has not remained shrouded in an inaccessible silence, but has spoken to men as to friends . . . to invite them and admit them to communion with him. The Revelation, therefore, far from reducing itself to a complex of truths pointed out to intelligence alone, is above all a proposal of communion and life. It is a story of salvation! The Creator placed himself with infinite tenderness at the pace of his own creations, introducing them progressively to an understanding of the mystery of his intimate life—I should say, the life of his heart—culminating in a complete manifestation in Jesus Christ, God's Word made flesh for the salvation of humanity.

To the women of our time, who seek, in a way that sometimes entails suffering, their true dignity, the All Beautiful One shows the great possibilities that female genius bears with it when it is pervaded by grace.

To little children and to youth, who look toward the future with anxious faith, remember that the Lord does not disappoint the deepest expectations of a person and comes to meet halfway those who wish to build a world of greater brotherhood and solidarity.

To those who are immersed in sin, but still yearn for the good, Our Lady of the Immaculate Conception points the way to real possibilities of redemption in the sincere quest for truth and in the faithful abandonment of oneself into the hands of the Lord.

ANGELUS
December 8, 1995

The angel spoke to Joseph on two occasions: "Rise, take the child and his mother, flee to Egypt, and stay there until I tell you. Herod is going to search for the child to destroy him" (Mt 2:13); and after the death of Herod: "Rise, take the child and his mother and go to the land of Israel" (Mt 2:19). In this account we can see two decisive moments for the Holy Family, first in Bethlehem when King Herod wants to kill the Child because he sees him as a rival for the throne; and in Egypt when, once the danger is over, the Holy Family can return from their exile to Nazareth. Let us observe first of all God's paternal concern—the divine concern of the Father for his Son Incarnate—and, in what is almost a mirror image, Joseph's human concern. At Joseph's side, we perceive the silent and anxious presence of Mary, who meditates in her heart over the concern of God and the obedient alacrity of Joseph.

ANGELUS
December 31, 1995

It is to children especially that we have dedicated the theme of World Peace Day, which we are celebrating today: "Let's give children a peaceful future!" The children of the Earth, at this end of the century, are the seeds of the third millennium: they ask for their future sprouts of peace, the inheritance of a world united in solidarity. May the world, which so badly needs peace, listen to their pleas! The little ones are the embodiment of the hopes, the expectations, and the potential of human partnership; they are witnesses and teachers of hope, a feeling that they experience with joyful enthusiasm. Let us not extinguish the hope that is in their hearts; let us not suffocate their expectations of peace!

ANGELUS
January 1, 1996

You are little children, and some a little older: let me wish you, first of all, a Happy New Year, because we are already four weeks into the new year. And now all of you, all of us are one year older: so if someone was born in 1995, now they are one year old, and if someone was born in 1920 like me, now they are seventy-six years old. So I wish you a good new year; but Happy New Year doesn't mean only one more number, it also means progress as the Gospel tells us—to progress in Jesus, who progressed in years, progressed in grace, and progressed in wisdom. I wish all this for you: to progress in years, in grace, and in wisdom. The catechism is very useful for this, the catechism in schools and in the parish. But the sacraments are also very important. You have all been baptized, many of you will receive this year your First Communion, and I hope that you will prepare successfully for that moment, which will help you later to continue along your path of sacramental.

SPEECH TO CHILDREN OF SAINT CLETUS POPE PARISH, ROME, ITALY
January 28, 1996

The Cross of Jesus has a value and a significance that still remain relevant and deeply alive, because it is from this trunk of wood that the fruit of the redemption springs unceasingly for all. In it are sunk the roots of the new life that at the same time offers us continual hopes and prospects. For that reason, we must replenish our faith with a continual meditation on the mystery of redemption that was attained once and for all on Golgotha.

Next to this moving image we see the Virgin Mary, the apostle John, and Mary Magdalene. They are witnesses to that sublime moment, and they invite us to remain in an attitude of faith and devotion at the side of the Cross from which comes our salvation.

SPEECH, ESQUIPULAS, GUATEMALA
February 6, 1996

I am deeply moved as I recall so many illustrious sons and daughters of Venezuela, and I issue my appeal to politicians that, by transcending their party differences and their particular interests, they might unite their will in a responsible and disinterested pursuit of the common good, with a particular eye to the less prosperous classes. In this difficult but decisive moment for the life of the nation, I exhort the politicians and those who hold high executive office to work tirelessly for the true good of the nation, effectively upholding the initiatives that encourage it and giving clear testimony of honesty in their private and professional lives.

SPEECH TO SOCIAL, CULTURAL, POLITICAL, AND ECONOMIC LEADERS, CARACAS, VENEZUELA
February 10, 1996

The backpack is a symbol of hiking. You have to hike if you want to carry anything with you in this backpack. I am a hiker, or at least I used to be. Today I am less so. Now I'm someone who travels by plane. Last week, last Sunday, I met a great many of the young people of Venezuela in Caracas. Now I bring you their greetings, and I hope that you too are in communion with the young people of Venezuela. This rainbow is a fine symbol. The rainbow is a sign of the covenant between God and humanity, and also of the covenant between humanity and its various components and among the various continents. We can imagine this rainbow linking Rome and Caracas. That is how I interpret it. And I thank you for this spiritual rainbow that you are trying to promote in your youthful community. Let us hope that other journeys can be taken with this backpack and that other rainbows will appear.

SPEECH TO YOUTH OF SAINT VINCENT PALLOTTI PARISH, ROME, ITALY
February 18, 1996

I have tried to walk with young people from the very first hours of my Petrine ministry here in Rome. But I did it before then, too, in Cracow. I remember October 22, 1978, a day when many of you were not yet born, when I said, after the celebration in Saint Peter's Square: "You are my hope." And it is true. This hope in the young accompanies me and, thanks be to God, the young people also accompany me. They accompany me in various places—in the parishes of Rome, my meetings with young people are indispensable—but also in meetings all over Italy, as in Loreto, and in the World Youth Days, which are so magnificent. Youth passes, we become adults and then old people. But something of youth always remains, an inner youth lives on. I feel young despite the years I carry with me. I remember when I was an altar boy. The Mass was different then. It began with the words "Introibo ad altare Dei" (I will go to the altar of God), and the altar boy responded: "Ad Deum qui laetificat iuventutem meam" (To God who gives joy to my youth). This is true. Joy comes from the Lord.

SPEECH TO YOUTH OF SAINT BIBIANA PARISH, ROME, ITALY
March 3, 1996

May the Lord grant you merit for your work — the Lord who, come to heal man, is the Divine Doctor whom every human being actually needs. In the course of his life on Earth, Jesus felt special compassion for those who suffered and took upon himself, with the Sacrifice of the Cross, all human pain and grief. Therefore, the face of Christ glows in a special way in sick people. Just as the Savior was moved in the presence of the sick people that he met, likewise it is just that we too should feel involved in the pain of our brothers and sisters, especially when they are children. And this is especially true of the innocent victims of many larger situations of suffering and emergencies. Children are the heart of humanity, the hope and the future of the world.

SPEECH TO ORGANIZERS OF MERCEDES-BENZ DEALERS' CAMPAIGN TO AID HIV-POSITIVE CHILDREN
March 4, 1996

Are you called Carlo? My first name is also Carlo, and so we belong to the same family, the family of all those whose name is Carlo. But did you work to build this church? You did? I imagine you worked very hard. But I tell you that you are still building this church. Because a church is not built with bricks alone; it is also and primarily built with living rocks. The living rocks are all those who have been baptized. You have been baptized and therefore you too are living rocks. With these living rocks we build a living Church, the Church inhabited by the Holy Spirit, the Church of Christ. I hope that you children will build the Church more and more, with your catechism, with your Christian behavior. You are the future, you are the future of the fatherland, of the Church, and of this parish for which we are today erecting a church. I thank you.

SPEECH TO CHILDREN OF THE BLESSED (NOW SAINT) JOSEMARÍA ESCRIVÁ PARISH, ROME, ITALY
March 10, 1996

Saint Joseph, a "righteous man," whom Divine Providence placed alongside Jesus and Mary to provide for the Holy Family with his daily labor, reminds us that the ways of salvation also pass through human work and invites us all to seize the opportunities it offers.

In performing his duty, Saint Joseph presents himself as a man capable of effecting a synthesis between faith and life, between the demands of God and those of man, between personal needs and the good of others.

I hope that, based on the example of so great a saint, every member of the working world feels called upon to encourage and organize harmonious development, justice, and solidarity.

SPEECH TO REPRESENTATIVES OF THE WORLD OF WORK, COLLE DI VAL D'ELSA, ITALY
March 30, 1996

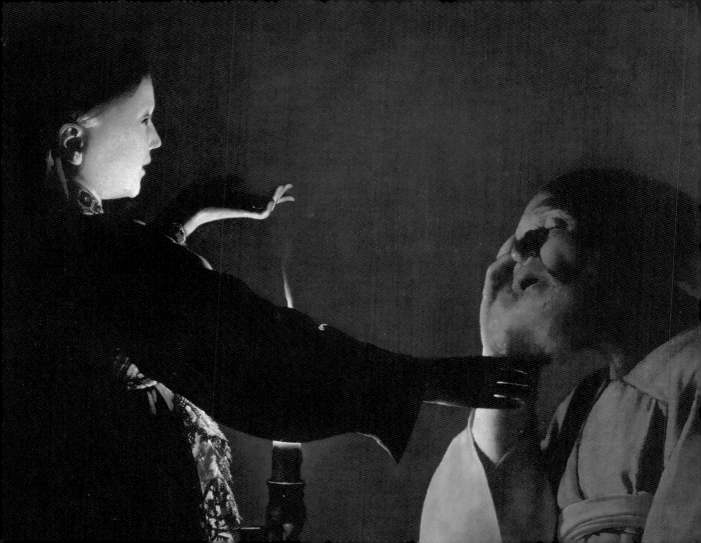

Because I am here in observance of the recent Feast Day of Saint Joseph, I would like to begin by repeating to you all the words that God, through his angel, sent to Saint Joseph: "Do not be afraid to take Mary as your wife!" (Mt 1:20). And I say to you: Do not be afraid to take Mary as your Mother in the journey of life! Let Mary be a model for you of how to follow Jesus. Do not be afraid to enter into confidence with her, to entrust to her maternal hands all problems, all concerns, all expectations and plans. Above all, confide in her the plan that concerns your entire life: the vocation, in the sincere commitment of all that you are, for the complete fulfillment of yourselves.

The Cross leads us spiritually to Calvary. With Mary we stand at the feet of the dying Christ. The Cross speaks to us of the mercy of God. Let us be won over by this boundless mercy that summons us, transfigures us, and saves us. It is the way to approach with respect and love the tragedy of the Son of God who offers his life for us. Beloved young people, may you know how to read in the Cross the measure of the love of God: a boundless measure! Turn your gaze toward the Crucifix and await in trepidation the message that he — the only one with the message of eternal life — sends out to everyone. From it draw the force to support and feed your testimony as disciples and messengers of the Gospel.

ANGELUS
March 31, 1996

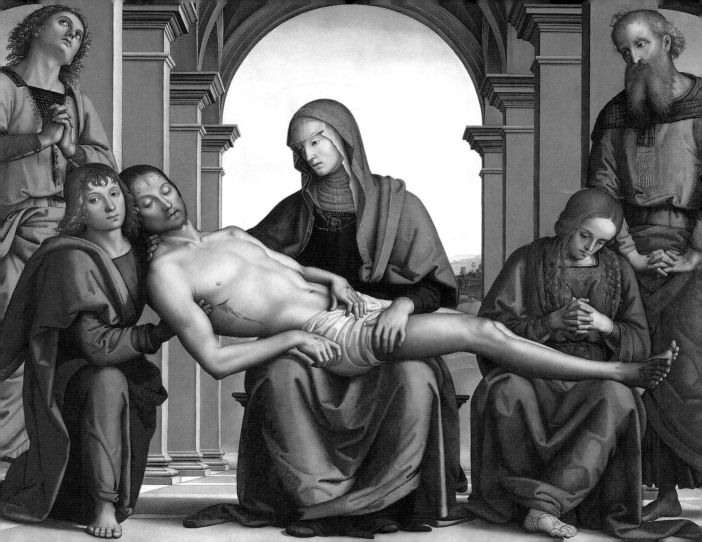

The Church is rapt in the contemplation of Christ risen. It thus relives the original experience that lies at the foundation of its existence. The Church feels overwhelmed by the same astonishment as the Magdalene and the other women who went to the tomb of Christ on Easter morning and found it empty. That sepulcher had become a womb of life. Those who had condemned Jesus had the illusion that they would be able to suffocate his cause beneath a cold tombstone. The disciples themselves had surrendered to a sense of irreparable failure. You can imagine their surprise, then, and even their mistrust, when they heard the news of the empty tomb.

But the Risen One did not delay in showing himself, and they acceded to reality. They saw and they believed! Two thousand years later, there still wells up the ineffable emotion that swept over them when they heard their Teacher greet them: "Peace to you!"

ANGELUS
April 21, 1996

You know through your own personal experience the importance, in the performance of your duties, of a sense of obligation and of solidarity toward your fellow citizens. You have learned to accept, like the centurion in the Gospel, your position as servants of the state and, at the same time, as guardians of public order. You are and you have been men of daily commitment, carrying out your mission with courage, even in the most challenging and delicate moments. How many stories of personal heroism are inscribed in the history of the Corps! There have even been those among the Carabinieri whose loyalty has cost them their lives. To you here today, to your fellow soldiers who have fallen in the line of duty, and to you, colleagues of the victims of duty, let me extend a special admiration and gratitude.

SPEECH TO THE NATIONAL ASSOCIATION OF CARABINIERI
June 1, 1996

Far from everyday life, which is often frantic and sometimes unfortunately alienating, in these lovely mountain localities we have a chance to rediscover in the beauty of creation the greatness of God and man, and we are invited to achieve a more complete harmony with the Creator of the universe. In the face of the majesty of the mountains, we are driven to establish a more respectful relationship with nature. At the same time, made more aware of the value of the cosmos, we are encouraged to meditate on the gravity of the many desecrations of the environment, all too often perpetrated with unacceptable recklessness. When contemporary man allows himself to be led astray by false myths, he loses sight of the riches and the hopes for life contained in creation, this astonishing gift of Divine Providence for all of humanity.

ANGELUS, LORENZAGO DI CODORE, ITALY
July 14, 1996

Vacations, therefore, should not be seen as a simple escape, which impoverishes and dehumanizes, but rather as defining moments in a person's very existence. By interrupting the daily rhythms, which exhaust us and weary us both physically and spiritually, they offer the possibility of recovering the most profound aspects of life and work. In moments of rest and, in particular, during the holidays, man is invited to become aware of the fact that work is a means and not the goal of life, and he has the possibility of discovering the beauty of silence as a space in which to find himself again by opening up to gratitude and prayer. It comes spontaneously to him, then, to consider his life and the lives of others with fresh eyes. Freed from the pressing pursuits of everyday life, he has a chance to discover his contemplative dimension, while recognizing the traces of God in nature and especially in other human beings. This is an experience, then, that opens him to a renewed attention to the people who live alongside him, beginning with his own family.

ANGELUS, PIEVE DI CADARE, ITALY
July 21, 1996

To all of you a sincere thank-you, and especially for the prayers! Great is the value of human suffering and indispensable is the contribution of the so-called "third age"! Sickness is a two-sided condition: on the one hand, it hinders people in various ways, leading them to experience limitations and fragility; on the other hand, by putting them in more direct contact with the Cross of Christ, it enriches them with new possibilities. With the offering to Christ of their own sufferings, the sick can provide a personal contribution to his work of redemption and participate actively in the edification of the Church. The elderly constitute a very precious presence for families and for society.

SPEECH TO THE SICK AND THE ELDERLY, PANNONHALMA, HUNGARY
September 6, 1996

As can be seen, before being a doctrine, Christianity is an "event," indeed, a Person: it is Jesus of Nazareth. He is the heart of the Christian faith. Hosts of saints, monks, and mystics have left everything to enjoy intimacy with him. But Christ can also be met on the world's highways. The great Dostoyevsky, in a letter recalling the incredulity and doubt that marked so many moments in his life, offers this moving witness: "Those are the moments when I composed a creed: to believe that there is nothing more beautiful, more profound, more loving, more reasonable, and more perfect than Christ, and that not only is there nothing but—I say it to myself with a jealous love—one cannot have anything" (letter to Madame Von Visine, February 20, 1854). In turn, Semen Frank, a recent Russian thinker, reflecting on the enigma of suffering, writes: "The idea of a God who came down into the world, who voluntarily suffers and shares in human and cosmic suffering, the idea of a God-man who suffers, is the only possible theodicy, the only convincing justification of God" (*Dieu est avec nous*, p. 195).

ANGELUS
September 15, 1996

"You are the salt of the Earth. . . . You are the light of the world."

What, then, is light? We discover it on the basis of experience: light glows and illuminates. It is thanks to light that our cities and our streets are not left in darkness. Light can be seen from a long way off: it dissipates the shadows and allows us to see the faces of others. It is pleasant to gather the family together in the evening, by the light of the hearth. With these images of salt and light, Christ speaks today to you families gathered here. Be the salt of the Earth! Be the light of the world! What does this mean? The Lord explains it to us: "Just so, your light must shine before others, that they may see your good deeds and glorify your heavenly Father" (Mt 5:16).

SPEECH TO YOUNG COUPLES AND THEIR CHILDREN, SAINTE-ANNE-D'AURAY, FRANCE
September 20, 1996

This is precisely why it is necessary to commit oneself to keeping one's heart open and attentive to what the heaven represents, that is, to God. Not in order to escape reality and its problems, but in order to give the soul "oxygen" and allow it to face life from God's perspective. To cultivate one's spiritual dimension, both personally and within the family, making room for silence, prayer, dialogue, and the strong components of the Sunday Eucharist and of the Sacrament of Reconciliation—these are the things that are made possible by flying ever higher, toward God, who is life, love, and never-ending peace.

SPEECH TO THE 31ST WING OF THE ITALIAN AIR FORCE, CASTEL GANDOLFO, ITALY
September 29, 1996

Fifty years after the blessed day in which the Holy Spirit, through the laying on of hands by the archbishop of Cracow, Adam Stefan Sapieha, consecrated me as a priest of Christ, I extend to God my deeply felt gratitude for what he has chosen to accomplish through me. At the same time, I extend my gratitude to the many people I have met along the way who, to varying degrees, helped me in my journey over these many years.

May the Everlasting Father, through the intercession of Mary, queen of all the saints, continue to guide my footsteps, that I may be a faithful minister of the divine gifts and a generous servant of the flock that he has entrusted to me.

SPEECH ON THE FIFTIETH ANNIVERSARY OF HIS ORDINATION
October 31, 1996

In the face of the transformations that have taken place in Poland, I wish to make your consciences particularly sensitive to the evangelical ideals of love, justice, and solidarity, which must guide every action for the present and the future. Without these values no authentic social order can exist. A society that wishes to define itself as democratic and free cannot function properly unless it respects the fundamental rights of man, and among them, the most fundamental right of all: the right to life from conception to natural death.

SPEECH TO REPRESENTATIVES OF THE POLISH LABOR UNION SOLIDARITY
November 11, 1996

In the analyses that were developed in preparation for your meeting, it is mentioned that more than eight hundred million still suffer from malnutrition and that it is often difficult to find immediate solutions to improve on a rapid basis such tragic conditions. All the same, we must work together to find those solutions, in order that there may no longer be, side by side, people who are starving and others who live in luxury, extremely poor people and extremely rich people, people who lack basic necessities and others who squander wantonly. Such contrasts between poverty and wealth are intolerable for mankind.

SPEECH TO THE WORLD SUMMIT ON NUTRITION, ROME, ITALY
November 13, 1996

Today, Rome is once again in Piazza di Spagna, at the foot of this column, to pay homage to the Holy Virgin, conceived without sin. Not only this piazza, but the whole city possesses an extraordinary level of natural and artistic beauty. In Rome the visitor encounters monuments of the ancient Roman empire, early Christian basilicas, buildings of the Renaissance and the Baroque period, Saint Peter's cathedral with its magnificent dome, so many museums abounding in sculptures and paintings, in which the genius of Italy has expressed itself over the centuries.

Does not this precious patrimony constitute a distant reflection of the beauty of God, the Highest Good and the Highest Beauty, to whom man, even without knowing it, reaches out with every fiber of his being?

In Mary this reflection becomes closer to us and more direct. Hers is an exquisitely spiritual beauty: the beauty of the Immaculate Conception, a unique and exclusive prerogative of the Virgin of Nazareth.

Non si possono saltare i giovani: I learned by heart this wordplay that your parish priest has repeated to me many times. A maxim that is worthy of a son of Don Bosco. "You cannot skip/leap over young people." And that is certainly true, in part because young people are better leapers than we are! Just look at all the balls here: young people are specialists in soccer, basketball — all the sports!

Young people are born leapers, and that is right; it is as it should be, Christ wants it this way, Saint Paul wants it this way, Don Bosco wants it this way, and we all want it this way.

With these leaps, we should think of a plan for life, because life is not merely our youth, but also maturity and then old age. These are all periods of life for which we much create a proper plan from our youth, that is the time when we must do it.

SPEECH TO YOUTH OF SAINT MARY OF HOPE PARISH, ROME, ITALY
January 19, 1997

Jesus's love for the sick encourages us especially to put the resources of our heart into action. We know from experience that, when we are ill, we not only need adequate treatment, but human warmth. Unfortunately, in contemporary society we often risk losing genuine contact with others. The pace of work, stress, or family crisis makes it increasingly difficult for us to give one another fraternal support. It is the weakest who pay the price. Thus it can happen that the elderly who are no longer self-sufficient, defenseless children, the disabled, the severely handicapped, and the terminally ill are sometimes seen as a burden and even an obstacle to be removed. On the other hand, walking at their side, dear brothers and sisters, helps build a society with a human face, enlivened by a deep sense of solidarity, where there is room and respect for all, especially the weakest.

ANGELUS
February 9, 1997

Dear brothers and sisters, let us look to Mary, the Virgin who listens, who was always prepared to welcome and to treasure in her heart her divine Son's every word (cf. Lk 2:51). The Gospel says: "Blessed are you who believed that what was spoken to you by the Lord would be fulfilled" (Lk 1:45). May the heavenly Mother of God help us enter into deep harmony with the Word of God so that Christ may become the light and guide of our whole life.

ANGELUS
February 23, 1997

In the Transfiguration the heavenly Father's voice is heard: "This is my beloved Son; listen to him" (Mk 9:7). These words contain the whole program for Lent: we must listen to Jesus. He reveals the Father to us, because, as the eternal Son, he is "the image of the invisible God" (Col 1:15). But at the same time, as true "Son of man," he reveals what we are, he reveals man to man (cf. *Gaudium et spes*, § 22). So let us not be afraid of Christ! In raising us to the heights of his divine life, he does not take away our humanity, but on the contrary, he humanizes us, giving our personal and social life full meaning.

ANGELUS
February 23, 1997

Jesus, the beginning and the fulfillment of the new man, convert our hearts so that, abandoning the ways of error, we walk in your footsteps on the path that leads to life. Make us live our faith steadfastly, fulfilling our baptismal promises, testifying with conviction to your word, that the life-giving light of the Gospel may shine in our families and in society.

Dear young people, I am expecting you in Paris, where it will give me great joy to meet you and share with you in prayer and in reflection our common faith in Christ, source of immortal life. From every corner of the world the Church sees advancing a new generation thirsting for truth, freedom, and happiness. Dear young people, you long for an interior life and dialogue with Christ. You seek authentic teachers and witnesses to show you the way of truth and love. You sometimes ask yourselves: "Who will teach us to pray? Who will introduce us into the life-giving mystery of the Good News?" Look at all those who have gone before you on the arduous and exciting path of faith and holiness. They will help you share that same witness to faith, which has marked their life.

ANGELUS
August 3, 1997

Let Christ dwell in your hearts! Entrust your ordeal to him! He will help you bear it. In secret and in silence, you can be united with the other young people who are meeting in Paris. Indeed, with your prayers, your sacrifices, your personal renewal, you share in the success of this great gathering and in your brothers' and sisters' conversion. Was it not by prayer alone that Saint Theresa of the Child Jesus made a prisoner's conversion possible, and without leaving her convent, did she not help the missionaries who struggled to proclaim the Gospel?

Dear young people, have trust! Be reconciled by Christ! May you obtain interior peace, the grace to repent, to be forgiven by God and, as you desire, to lead a better life from now on! With the help of your families, your friends, and the Church, I hope you will return to your place in society, where you will be concerned to work at the service of your brothers and sisters, with respect for their persons and their possessions.

MESSAGE TO YOUNG FRENCH PRISONERS, PARIS, FRANCE
August 22, 1997

I therefore say to you: at the crossroads where the many paths of your days intersect, question yourselves about the truth value of every choice you make. It can sometimes happen that the decision is difficult or hard and that there is an insistent temptation to give in. This had happened to Jesus's disciples, for the world is full of easy and inviting ways, downhill roads that plunge into the shadow of the valley where the horizon becomes more and more limited and stifling. Jesus offers you an uphill road, which is heavy going but lets the eye of the heart sweep over ever broader horizons. The choice is yours: to let yourselves slide downhill into the valley of a dull conformism, or to face the effort of climbing to the peak, where you can breathe the pure air of truth, goodness, and love.

SPEECH TO YOUTH, BOLOGNA, ITALY
September 27, 1997

It is not true that married couples, as though slaves condemned to their own weakness, cannot be faithful to their total gift of self until death! May the Lord, who calls you to live in the unity of "one flesh," a unity of body and soul, a unity of the whole of life, give you the strength for a fidelity that ennobles you and ensures that your union will not run the risk of betrayal, which robs it of dignity and happiness and brings division and sorrow to the home, the chief victims of which are the children. The best protection for the family is fidelity, which is a gift of the faithful and merciful God, in a love redeemed by him.

I am pleased to recall what Pope Paul VI wrote in his apostolic exhortation *Marialis cultus*: "As a Gospel prayer centered on the mystery of the redemptive Incarnation, the Rosary is therefore a prayer with a clearly Christological orientation. Its most characteristic element, in fact, the litany-like succession of Hail Marys, . . . constitutes the warp on which is woven the contemplation of the mysteries . . . as seen through the eyes of her who was closest to the Lord" (§ 46–47).

How many times in the course of history has the Church had recourse to this prayer, especially in particularly difficult moments. The Holy Rosary was a privileged means for averting the danger of war and obtaining the gift of peace from God. Did not the Blessed Virgin, when appearing to the three shepherd children in Fátima eighty years ago, ask that the Rosary be recited for the conversion of sinners and for peace in the world?

ANGELUS
October 26, 1997

L·LOTVS·MDXXXIX

"Man sees the appearance, but the Lord looks into the heart" (1 Sm 16:7). And Mary's heart was fully disposed to the fulfillment of the divine will. This is why the Blessed Virgin is the model of Christian expectation and hope.

In contemplating the biblical scene of the Annunciation, we understand that the divine message does not catch Mary unprepared; on the contrary, it finds her watching and waiting, recollected in profound silence, in which echo the promises of the prophets of Israel, especially Isaiah's famous messianic prophecy: "The virgin shall be with child, and bear a son, and shall name him Immanuel" (7:14).

In her heart there is no shade of selfishness; she desires nothing for herself except God's glory and human salvation.

ANGELUS
December 8, 1997

I have come to Cuba as a messenger of truth and life, to bring you the Good News, to proclaim to you "the love of God in Christ Jesus, our Lord" (Rom 8:39). This love alone can light up the night of human loneliness; this love alone can strengthen the hope of all who search for happiness.

Christ has told us, "No one has greater love than this, to lay down one's life for one's friends. You are my friends if you do what I command you. . . . I have called you friends" (Jn 15:13–15). Christ offers you his friendship. He gave his life so that those who wish to answer his call can indeed become his friends. His is a friendship that is deep, genuine, loyal, and total, as all true friendship must be.

MESSAGE TO CUBAN YOUTH, CAMAGÜEY, CUBA
January 23, 1998

This is the true meaning and value of suffering, of the pain that is physical, moral, and spiritual. This is the Good News that I wish to pass on to you. To our human questioning, the Lord responds with a call, with a special vocation that is grounded in love. Christ comes to us not with explanations and reasons that might either anaesthetize or alienate us. Instead, he comes to us saying, "Come with me. Follow me on the way of the Cross. The Cross is suffering." "If anyone wishes to come after me, he must deny himself and take up his cross daily and follow me" (Lk 9:23). Jesus Christ has taken the lead on the way of the Cross. He has suffered first. He does not drive us toward suffering but shares it with us, wanting us to have life and to have it in abundance (cf. Jn 10:10).

MEETING WITH THE SICK, LA HABANA, CUBA
January 24, 1998

Dear Christian families, look to the need for love, giving, and openness to life that is present in the hearts of your children, disoriented by the sight of failed marriages. The children learn to love their own husband or wife by watching the example of their parents. Do not be content to live the Gospel of the family only internally; announce it and testify to it to everyone you meet along your way and in every walk of public and social life.

SPEECH FOR THE FESTIVAL OF THE FAMILY, ROME, ITALY
February 2, 1998

Spurred by love, Christ suffered willingly and as an innocent man, thus proving the truth of love through the truth of suffering, a suffering that he, the God-man, experienced with incomparable intensity. But precisely through this sacrifice, he joined suffering to love once and for all, and in this way redeemed it.

277

ANGELUS
February 8, 1998

Promoting the authentic, balanced, overall health of women means helping them to harmonize their physical, psychological, and social well-being with moral and spiritual values. In this perspective of personal and specifically feminine fulfillment, in which spousal and maternal self-giving is lived in the family or in consecrated life and a sense of social solidarity is expressed, health represents both a fundamental condition and a dimension of the person.

When Jesus, as the Gospels attest, addressed the crucial question to his disciples: "But who do you say that I am?" (Mt 16:15), it was Simon Peter who replied, "You are the Messiah, the Son of the living God" (Mt 16:16). On that day Christ recognized the special charism given by the Father to the fisherman of Galilee, the charism of sincere and solid faith. For this reason he called him Cephas, which in Hebrew means "rock," and promised that on this faith he would build his Church (cf. Mt 16:17–18).

Down the centuries and also today, on the threshold of the third millennium, Peter in the person of his successors is called to confess and proclaim that Jesus is the Christ, the Savior.

ANGELUS
February 22, 1998

The human genome in a way is the last continent to be explored. In this millennium now drawing to a close, so full of tragedies and achievements, people have come to know each other and in some ways have grown closer as a result of geographical explorations and discoveries. Human knowledge has also made important advances in the world of physics, to the point of recently discovering the structure of atomic particles. Through the knowledge of genetics and molecular biology, scientists can look with the penetrating gaze of science into the inner fabric of life and the mechanisms that characterize individuals, thus ensuring the continuity of living species.

These advances increasingly reveal the Creator's greatness, because they allow man to discover the intrinsic order of Creation and to appreciate the wonders of his body, in addition to his intellect, which to a certain extent reflects the light of the Word through whom "all things came to be" (Jn 1:3).

SPEECH TO THE PONTIFICAL ACADEMY FOR LIFE
February 24, 1998

We are unfortunately heirs to a history of enormous conditioning that has hindered the progress of women: their dignity is sometimes ignored, their special qualities misrepresented, and they themselves are frequently marginalized. This has prevented them from being truly themselves and has deprived the whole human race of authentic spiritual riches.

How many women have been and are still valued more for their physical appearance than for their personal qualities, professional competence, intellectual work, the richness of their sensitivity, and, finally, for the very dignity of their being!

May Mary, the model of a fulfilled woman, help everyone, especially all women, to understand the "feminine genius," not only to carry out God's precise plan, but also to make more room for women in the various areas of social life.

As I took my leave of you sixteen years ago, I addressed my final words to the children of Nigeria, reminding them that they are loved by God and that they reflect the love of God. Those children are now grown up, and many of them have children of their own; but the message I leave today is the same as I left then. The children and young people of Africa must be protected from the terrible hardships visited upon the thousands of innocent victims who are forced to become refugees, who are left hungry, or who are mercilessly abducted, abused, enslaved, or killed. We must all work for a world in which no child will be deprived of peace and security, of a stable family life, of the right to grow up without fear and anxiety.

FAREWELL CEREMONY, NNAMDI AZIKIWE AIRPORT, NIGERIA
March 23, 1998

Spirit of life, by whose power the Word was made flesh
In the womb of the Virgin Mary, the woman of attentive silence,
Make us docile to the promptings of your love,
And ever ready to accept the signs of the times
That you place along the paths of history.

There is a need for Christian forgiveness, which instills hope and trust without weakening the struggle against evil. There is a need to give and receive mercy.

But we cannot forgive if we do not let God forgive us first, recognizing that it is we who are the object of his mercy. We will be ready to forgive the debts of others only if we become aware of the enormous debt that we ourselves have been forgiven.

The Christian people call upon Mary as Mother of Mercy. In her, God's merciful love became incarnate and her Immaculate Heart is always and everywhere a safe refuge for sinners.

ANGELUS
March 29, 1998

Down the centuries, the Cross has been embraced by many Christians: how can we not give thanks to God for this? And you, young people of Rome, you are witnesses of how, during the City Mission too, the message of Death and Resurrection that comes from the Cross becomes a proclamation of hope that overwhelms and consoles, strengthens the spirit and makes hearts peaceful. How appropriate Jesus's words sound: "And when I am lifted up from the Earth, I will draw everyone to myself" (Jn 12:32) and "they will look upon him whom they have pierced" (Jn 19:37)!

The angel invites us not to seek the living among the dead. We can gather two teachings from his words. First of all, the exhortation never to tire of seeking the risen Christ, who gives abundant life to those who meet him. Finding Christ means discovering peace of heart, as the experience of so many converts attests. The women in the Gospel, after their initial experience, feel deep joy at finding the Teacher alive (cf. Mt 28:8–9). I hope that all will have the same spiritual experience, welcoming into their hearts, their homes, and their families the joyful message of Easter: "Christ now raised from the dead will never die again; death no longer has power over him, alleluia" (Communion antiphon).

Jesus appeared to the apostles in the upper room and said to them, "Receive the Holy Spirit. Whose sins you forgive are forgiven them, whose sins you retain are retained" (Jn 20:22–23). With these words the risen Christ calls the apostles to be messengers and ministers of his merciful love, and from that day, from generation to generation, this proclamation of hope has resounded in the heart of the Church for every believer. Blessed are those who open their hearts to divine mercy! The Lord's merciful love precedes and accompanies every act of evangelization and enriches it with extraordinary fruits of conversion and spiritual renewal.

ANGELUS
April 19, 1998

We are also told in the Acts of the Apostles that the Mother of the Risen One was present at the center of the newborn apostolic community: "All these devoted themselves with one accord to prayer, together with the some women and Mary, the mother of Jesus, and his brothers" (Acts 1:14).

Just as she was intimately joined at the foot of the Cross to Christ's redeeming sacrifice, so Mary is the silent witness among the apostles in the upper room. In a certain sense, she enlivens their faith and their prayer. She supports and encourages them, as with one voice they call upon the Holy Spirit promised by Jesus. This image of the first community at prayer, in expectation of Pentecost, must always remain before our eyes, especially in this year dedicated to the Holy Spirit, in order to sustain our journey of faith and apostolate.

ANGELUS
April 26, 1998

You are not alone in this demanding journey of human and Christian formation, because Franciscan Youth is by its nature a vocation to grow in fraternity. By following Francis's original insight, you are well aware that a context in which people live as brothers and sisters encourages and spurs each one to open himself to his neighbor, making the most of his own potential. At the same time, he can receive the friendship and support of others. A central element of your Franciscan identity, therefore, is the presence of the brother to be welcomed, listened to, forgiven, and loved: in his face you, like Francis, must recognize that of Christ, especially when dealing with those who are least and lowliest.

With the image of God resting, the Bible indicates the Creator's joyful pleasure in the work of his hands. On the "seventh day" God turns to look at man and the world with admiration and love, a sentiment that is confirmed throughout salvation history, when the Creator, especially in the Exodus events, becomes the Savior of his people.

Thus, the "Lord's Day" is the day that shows God's love for his creatures. The prophets are not afraid to extol this relationship of love in marital terms (cf. Hos 2:16–24; Jer 2:2): from being the Creator, God became the "bridegroom" of humanity, and the Incarnation of his Son would be the high point of this mystical union.

ANGELUS
July 12, 1998

Today Mary seems even closer to us; from heaven she sees us and protects us. Contemplation of paradise does not distance us from the Earth; indeed, on the contrary, it is an incentive to us to work with all our might to transform our world in view of eternity. In our minds resounds the apostle's invitation to "seek what is above" (Col 3:1), where an eternal dwelling place is prepared for us in the common house of the Father.

A day of joy! Can joy be planned? Is this not a feeling that depends on the happy or sorrowful circumstances of life? In fact, genuine Christian joy cannot be reduced to a chance feeling: its foundations lie in the love God manifested to us in the Death and Resurrection of his Son.

This certainty gives us a profound reason to live and to hope. With their lives, the saints attest that we can experience deep joy even in conditions of physical and spiritual suffering, if we know we are surrounded by God's love.

ANGELUS
August 16, 1998

Dear young people, do not doubt the love that God feels for you! He holds a place in his heart and a mission in the world for you. Your first reaction may be fear or doubt. These are emotions that Jeremiah himself experienced before you: "Ah, Lord God! I know not how to speak; I am too young" (1:6). The task seems immense, because it takes on the dimensions of society and the world. But do not forget that, when he calls, the Lord also grants the strength and the grace necessary to answer the call.

Faith and reason are like two wings on which the human spirit rises to the contemplation of truth; and God has placed in the human heart a desire to know the truth—in a word, to know himself—so that, by knowing and loving God, men and women may also come to the fullness of truth about themselves.

ENCYCLICAL FIDES ET RATIO, OPENING BLESSING
September 14, 1998

When the meeting between divine Revelation and the modern media is conducted with respect for the truth of the biblical message and the correct use of technical means, it bears abundant good fruits. On the one hand, it means elevating the mass media to one of its noblest tasks, which in some way redeems it from improper and sometimes trivializing uses. On the other, it offers new and extraordinarily effective possibilities for introducing the general public to God's Word, communicated for the salvation of all mankind.

SPEECH TO THE CONFERENCE ON BIBLICAL LANGUAGE AND CONTEMPORARY COMMUNICATION
September 28, 1998

So, how old will you be in 2000? And how old will the Pope be? Eighty, that's right! The Pope was born in 1920. . . . Thanks be to God! We are thankful for this period that still reminds us of the birthday of the Lord, we are thankful for our own birthday, and for all the graces that God has given us during our life: whether the life is still short; a life of some days, months, or years; or whether it is fairly long, like the life of someone who is eighty years old. I commend myself to your prayers, because an older man has all the more need of help from young people. And so I commend myself to your prayers, and I am thankful for the opportunity to meet you, not only you children, but also your parents, your catechists, your parish priest, and all those who are here.

I feel very close to each one of those suffering, as well as to the doctors and other health-care professionals who offer their selfless service to the sick. I would like my voice to transcend these walls to bring Christ's voice to all the sick and to all health-care workers, and to offer in this way a word of comfort in their illness and of encouragement in the mission of assistance, recalling in particular the value of suffering within the framework of the Savior's redemptive work.

To be with you, to serve you with love and skill, is not only a humanitarian and social work, but above all an eminently evangelical activity, since Christ himself invites us to imitate the Good Samaritan, who, on seeing the suffering man on the wayside, did not pass by "on the opposite side" but "was moved with compassion . . . approached the victim, poured oil and wine over his wounds and bandaged them . . . and cared for him" (Lk 10:32–34).

MESSAGE TO THE SICK, MEXICO CITY, MEXICO
January 24, 1999

It is the school's task to develop in the students an appropriate knowledge of the world, of cultures and of languages, and at the same time to help them search for the truth with an open mind, in order to form a free and responsible personality. In this journey that nourishes the mind, acceptance of the "mystery" of man cannot be lacking: it appeals to God and makes us discover his action in the world.

It is necessary to promote educational and cultural projects suited to the full development of the person, which remains the central focus of the school and to which programs, interventions, and initiatives must be directed. In this way the school becomes a community that teaches one to search for the truth and to understand one's own personal dignity; that transmits culture and values for life; that trains one for a profession in the service of society; that opens one to encounter and to interpersonal and community dialogue; that responds to the demands for the human and spiritual, cultural and social growth of children and young people.

SPEECH TO STUDENTS, TEACHERS, AND SCHOOL ADMINISTRATORS, ROME, ITALY
February 13, 1999

Today, I am thinking in a special way of those who are still looking for their first position. For many young people, unemployment creates situations of anxiety and, sometimes, deep disappointment. They see themselves barred de facto from assuming direct responsibility in society and are often forced to delay starting a family. If this situation lasts too long, it becomes dangerous and unbearable, creating a barrier between individuals and society, and gives rise to a sense of distrust, which does not help the development of a civic consciousness.

SPEECH TO WORKERS OF MUNICIPAL ENTERPRISES, ROME, ITALY
March 19, 1999

For Christians, the basis of human dignity is found in God's love for each person, without exception; and true peace is a gift constantly offered and constantly received. Despite the violence and the many threats to life that our world is experiencing, during this year, which Catholics have dedicated to God the Father of mercies, the Church wishes to proclaim a message of hope in the future of mankind. She urgently invites all people of goodwill to join fearlessly in building the "civilization of love, founded on the universal values of peace, solidarity, justice, and liberty" (cf. Apostolic letter, *Tertio millennio adveniente*, § 52), and never to lose heart in the face of obstacles or setbacks.

SPEECH TO NOBEL PEACE PRIZE LAUREATES
April 22, 1999

I especially greet you, boys and girls, who are the real champions of the Spring Marathon. The word "spring" suggests the reawakening of nature and the desire to live; the word "marathon" recalls the dynamism of change and growth. These are the characteristic features of youth. May this happy event, which brings a message of trust and brotherhood through the city's streets, help to create a world where violence is banned and solidarity and peace prevail.

SPEECH TO PARTICIPANTS OF THE CATHOLIC SCHOOLS ASSOCIATION OF ROME SPRING MARATHON
April 24, 1999

It is necessary to harmonize the demands of the economy with those of ethics. At a deeper and more radical level, it is urgent and necessary to recognize, safeguard, and promote the indisputable primacy of the human person. An economy truly worthy of the name must be planned and achieved with respect for all the values and requirements of each and every human person and with a view to solidarity. In this regard, as I have more than once recalled, it is becoming urgent to act so that the economy, while retaining its legitimate autonomy, can be coordinated with the demands of a public policy essentially ordered to the common good. This also implies the search for suitable juridical instruments for an effective supranational "management" of the economy: corresponding to an international economic community should be an international civil society, capable of expressing forms of economic and political subjectivity inspired by solidarity and the quest for the common good in an ever widening vision that embraces the whole world.

SPEECH TO STUDENTS AND FACULTY OF BOCCONI UNIVERSITY, MILAN, ITALY
November 20, 1999

Allow me to tell you that I understand your aspirations and the challenges that you encounter. Unlike the generations that went before you, especially the generations that in their youth experienced the hardships linked to the World War and other conflicts, most of you were able to grow up in a climate of peace, liberty, and security. And yet you know from experience that material well-being does not automatically produce happiness and serenity. Nor does the liberty guaranteed by law suffice to make one feel free inside, in the depth of one's heart. Feedom from the slavery of passions springs from the regenerating power of Grace.

Human beings need Christ. Only in the encounter with him can be found the full truth of oneself. To follow Christ—as you know very well—demands generosity and boldness. But it is in his footsteps that one attains full self-realization and true liberty.

SPEECH TO YOUTH PREPARING FOR THE JUBILEE
November 21, 1999

The cinema enjoys a wealth of languages, a multiplicity of styles, and a variety of narrative forms that are truly great: from realism to fable, from history to science fiction, from adventure to tragedy, from comedy to news, from animated cartoon to documentary. It thus offers an incomparable storehouse of expressive means for portraying the various areas in which the human being finds himself and for interpreting his inescapable calling to the beautiful, the universal, and the absolute.

The cinema can thus help to bring distant people together, to reconcile enemies, to promote a more respectful and fruitful dialogue between different cultures, by showing the way to a credible and lasting solidarity, the essential premise for a world of peace. We know how much man also needs peace to be a true artist, to create true cinema!

SPEECH TO THE INTERNATIONAL CINEMA CONFERENCE ORGANIZED
BY THE PONTIFICAL COUNCIL FOR CULTURE
December 2, 1999

You offer the community a far-from-easy, but indispensable, service, using all your energies to ensure orderly conduct in urban life. Thanks to you, the residents of the city and the surrounding areas are helped to respect the laws that provide for a peaceful and harmonious society; the disadvantaged and minors can find helpful assistance in their difficulties; the environment, public and private property are safeguarded, and your continual work of prevention is an important safeguard of the citizens' well-being. You also facilitate the relations of individuals with the municipal authorities and their offices. At particular moments of difficulty, your presence becomes a vehicle for the effective solidarity of the entire community.

SPEECH AT THE JUBILEE OF THE ITALIAN MUNICIPAL POLICE
January 20, 2000

Mary guides and lights our way, dear brothers and sisters, whom I greet with great affection. Mary, our most tender Mother, accompanies us in joy and in sorrow, in good times and in those of physical and spiritual trial, in order to help us in every circumstance to say our yes to God's will. This morning in Saint Peter's Square we celebrated the Jubilee of the Sick and Health-Care Workers. This evening we have returned to ask Mary, "Health of the Sick," to make the Holy Year a true "year of grace." May the Immaculate Virgin help everyone to experience, "through sincere conversion of heart, the abundance of God's mercy and the joy of a fuller communion with their brothers and sisters, the first fruits of endless joy in heaven" (Prayer to Mary, Health of the Sick).

Viewed from the outside, [Michelangelo's dome] seems to outline the embrace of heaven over the community gathered in prayer, as if to symbolize God's love in drawing near to it. But when seen from the inside with its dizzying height, it suggests the fascination and effort required to rise to the full encounter with God.

Today's Jubilee celebration calls you, dear artists, precisely to rise in this way. It invites you to practice the wonderful "art" of holiness. If this should seem too difficult, may the thought that we are not alone on this journey give you comfort. Grace also sustains us through that ecclesial companionship in which the Church becomes a mother to each of us, obtaining from her divine bridegroom a superabundance of mercy and gifts. Is this not the meaning of the "mater Ecclesia" that Bernini powerfully depicted in the solemn embrace of the colonnade? Those majestic arms are always motherly arms reaching out to all humanity. Welcomed into them, every member of the Church can feel heartened on his pilgrim journey to our homeland.

SPEECH AT THE JUBILEE OF ARTISTS
February 18, 2000

God of our fathers,
you chose Abraham and his descendants
to bring your Name to the Nations:
we are deeply saddened by the behavior of those
who in the course of history
have caused these children of yours to suffer,
and asking your forgiveness we wish to commit ourselves
to genuine brotherhood
with the people of the Covenant.

PRAYER AT THE WESTERN WALL, JERUSALEM
March 26, 2000

Through personal and community prayer, through the sacraments, through the conversations you may have and through visiting significant places of the Church's history and Rome's artistic treasures, you will know Christ and his Church better and will find the way to bear witness to the Good News among your friends. May you be the witnesses that the new century so needs! Of course, you will sometimes need courage and daring to swim against the tide of the tempting offerings of today's world and to act in conformity with the Gospel demands of true love. But you will discover that life with Christ, the search for truth, the practice of fundamental human and moral values, respect for yourselves and for others lead to genuine freedom and true happiness. To achieve your ideals, ask adults to show you the way and to help you make progress!

SPEECH TO YOUTH ON PILGRIMAGE FROM THE ARCHDIOCESE OF ROUEN, FRANCE
April 14, 2000

May Jesus draw near to each one of us; may he become for us too a companion on the road! As he walks with us, he will explain that it was for our sake that he went to Calvary, for us that he died, in fulfillment of the Scriptures. Thus the sorrowful event of the Crucifixion, which we have just meditated upon, will become for each of us an eloquent lesson.

Dear brothers and sisters! The people of today need to meet Christ crucified and risen!

Who, if not the condemned Savior, can fully understand the pain of those unjustly condemned?

Who, if not the King scorned and humiliated, can meet the expectations of the countless men and women who live without hope or dignity?

Who, if not the crucified Son of God, can know the sorrow and loneliness of so many lives shattered and without a future?

SPEECH AT THE END OF THE WAY OF THE CROSS AT THE COLOSSEUM, ROME, ITALY
April 21, 2000

When sports are played and understood in the right way, they are an extraordinary expression of a person's best inner energies and of his ability to overcome difficulties, to set himself goals to be reached through sacrifice, generosity, and determination in facing the difficulties of competition.

Outstanding examples of all this are the noble athletes who have made cycling a great sport in Italy and in the world. At this time our thoughts naturally turn to Gino Bartali—recently deceased, a great sportsman, an exemplary citizen, and a convinced believer. His example continues to be a reference point for everyone of how sport can be practiced with great human and spiritual energy, making it a shining expression of the highest values of life and of social harmony.

I have come among you today as a witness to the risen Jesus. He knows what it is to suffer; he experienced the anguish of death, but by his Death he destroyed death itself and is absolutely the first human being to have freed himself from its chains once and for all. He traveled man's whole journey to the heavenly homeland, where he has prepared a throne of glory for each of us.

Dear sick brother or sister!

If someone or something makes you think that you have reached the end of the line, do not believe it! If you know the eternal love who created you, you also know that there is an immortal soul within you. There are various seasons in life; if by chance you feel winter approaching, I want you to know that it is not the last season, because the last one will be spring: the springtime of the Resurrection. Your whole life extends infinitely beyond its earthly limits: heaven awaits you.

GREETING TO THE SICK AT FÁTIMA, PORTUGAL
May 13, 2000

I send my cordial greetings to the participants in this spectacular event that sees athletes, artists, politicians, and dignitaries of Italian, Israeli, and Palestinian cultures meeting at Rome's Olympic Stadium for a friendly and extraordinary "Match of the Heart." I express my appreciation of this remarkable initiative, which aims at strengthening the culture of acceptance and dialogue among the Italian, Israeli, and Palestinian peoples.

Sports, a stimulating vehicle of human and moral values, can also help the world to be more fraternal and united. May this "Match of the Heart" encourage you, dear friends from different nations and cultures, to know one another better and to advance on the path of mutual respect and reciprocal esteem. In this friendly match may solidarity and peace be the real winners.

In this way may your message of hope be spread from the Olympic Stadium: Sports too can help build peace.

MESSAGE ON THE OCCASION OF THE MATCH OF THE HEART
May 25, 2000

"The heavens declare the glory of God; the sky proclaims its builder's craft" (Ps 19:1); with these words the psalmist evokes the "silent account" of the Creator's marvelous work inscribed in the reality of Creation itself.

God loves to make himself heard in the silence of Creation, in which the intellect senses the transcendence of the Lord of Creation. Everyone who seeks to understand the secrets of Creation and the mysteries of man must be ready to open their mind and heart to the deep truth which manifests itself there, and which "draws the intellect to give its consent" (Saint Albert the Great, *Commentary on John*, 6:44).

As something gratuitous, art reminds us that man and society cannot be reduced to efficiency at all costs. Cultural assets have the precise function of opening people to the meaning of the mystery and the revelation of the absolute, for they bear a message. For its part, religious art proclaims the divine in its own way and prepares the soul for contemplation of the Christian mysteries, by making understood through symbolic expression what words have great difficulty in expressing and by inviting Trinitarian prayer and devotion to the saints.

SPEECH TO THE INTERNATIONAL UNION OF INSTITUTES OF ARCHAEOLOGY, HISTORY, AND ART HISTORY, ROME, ITALY
May 26, 2000

The Good Shepherd is always going in search of the lost sheep, and when he finds them he puts them on his shoulders and brings them back to the flock. Christ is in search of every human being, whatever the situation!

This is because Jesus wants to save each one. And with a salvation that is offered, not imposed. What Christ is looking for is trusting acceptance, an attitude that opens the mind to generous decisions aimed at rectifying the evil done and fostering what is good. Sometimes this involves a long journey, but always a stimulating one, for it is a journey not made alone, but in the company of Christ himself and with his support. Jesus is a patient traveling companion, who respects the seasons and rhythms of the human heart. He never tires of encouraging each person along the path to salvation.

MESSAGE FOR THE JUBILEE IN PRISONS
July 9, 2000

Dear friends who have traveled so many miles in so many ways to come to Rome, to the Tombs of the Apostles, let me begin by putting to you a question: what have you come here to find? You have come to celebrate your Jubilee, the Jubilee of the young Church. Yours is not just any journey. If you have set out on pilgrimage, it is not just for the sake of recreation or an interest in culture. Well, then, let me ask again: What have you come in search of? Or, rather, who have you come here to find?

There can be only one answer to that: you have come in search of Jesus Christ! But Jesus Christ has first gone in search of you. To celebrate the Jubilee can have no other meaning than that of celebrating and meeting Jesus Christ, the Word who took flesh and came to dwell among us.

In opening your Jubilee, dear young people, I would like to repeat the words with which I began my ministry as bishop of Rome and pastor of the universal Church; I would like them to guide your days in Rome: "Do not be afraid! Open, indeed, open wide the doors to Christ!" Open your hearts, your lives, your doubts, your difficulties, your joys, and your affections to his saving power, and let him enter your hearts. "Do not be afraid! Christ knows what is in man. He alone knows it." I said this on October 22, 1978. I repeat it with the same conviction, with the same force today, seeing the hope of the Church and of the world shining in your eyes. Yes, let Christ govern your young lives; serve him with love. To serve Christ is freedom!

Dear friends, to believe in Jesus today, to follow Jesus as Peter, Thomas, and the first apostles and witnesses did, demands of us, just as it did in the past, that we take a stand for him, almost to the point at times of a new martyrdom, the martyrdom of those who, today as yesterday, are called to go against the tide in order to follow the divine Master, to "follow the Lamb wherever he goes" (Rev 14:4). It is not by chance, dear young people, that I wanted the witnesses to the faith in the twentieth century to be remembered at the Colosseum during this Holy Year.

Perhaps you will not have to shed your blood, but you will certainly be asked to be faithful to Christ! A faithfulness to be lived in the circumstances of everyday life. I am thinking of how difficult it is in today's world for engaged couples to be faithful to purity before marriage. I think of how the mutual fidelity of young married couples is put to the test. I think of friendships and how easily the temptation to be disloyal creeps in.

PRAYER VIGIL FOR WORLD YOUTH DAY XV, UNIVERSITY OF ROME TOR VERGATA, ROME, ITALY
August 19, 2000

It is Jesus, in fact, that you seek when you dream of happiness; he is waiting for you when nothing else you find satisfies you; he is the beauty to which you are so attracted; it is he who provokes you with that thirst for fullness that will not let you settle for compromise; it is he who urges you to shed the masks of a false life; it is he who reads in your hearts your most genuine choices, the choices that others try to stifle. It is Jesus who stirs in you the desire to do something great with your lives, the will to follow an ideal, the refusal to allow yourselves to be ground down by mediocrity, the courage to commit yourselves humbly and patiently to improving yourselves and society, making the world more human and more fraternal.

PRAYER VIGIL FOR WORLD YOUTH DAY XV, UNIVERSITY OF ROME TOR VERGATA, ROME, ITALY
August 19, 2000

Around you, you hear all kinds of words. But only Christ speaks words that stand the test of time and remain for all eternity. The time of life that you are living calls for decisive choices on your part: decisions about the direction of your studies, about work, about your role in society and in the Church. It is important to realize that among the many questions surfacing in your minds, the decisive ones are not about "what." The basic question is "who": "who" am I to go to, "who" am I to follow, "to whom" should I entrust my life?

In the course of the century now past, young people like you were summoned to huge gatherings to learn the ways of hatred; they were sent to fight against one another. The various godless messianic systems that tried to take the place of Christian hope have shown themselves to be truly horrendous. Today you have come together to declare that in the new century you will not let yourselves be made into tools of violence and destruction; you will defend peace, paying the price in your person if need be. You will not resign yourselves to a world where other human beings die of hunger, remain illiterate, and have no work. You will defend life at every moment of its development; you will strive with all your strength to make this Earth ever more livable for all people.

PRAYER VIGIL FOR WORLD YOUTH DAY XV, UNIVERSITY OF ROME TOR VERGATA, ROME, ITALY
August 19, 2000

You are thinking about love and the choices it entails, and I imagine that you agree: what is really important in life is the choice of the person who will share it with you. But be careful! Every human person has inevitable limits. Even in the most successful of marriages there is always a certain amount of disappointment. So then, dear friends, does not this confirm what we heard the apostle Peter say? Every human being finds himself sooner or later saying what he said, "To whom shall we go? You have the words of eternal life." Only Jesus of Nazareth, the Son of God and of Mary, the eternal Word of the Father born two thousand years ago at Bethlehem in Judaea, is capable of satisfying the deepest aspirations of the human heart.

Today we wish to entrust to you the future that awaits us,
and we ask you to be with us on our way.
We are the men and women of an extraordinary time,
exhilarating yet full of contradictions.
Humanity now has instruments of unprecedented power:
we can turn this world into a garden,
or reduce it to a pile of rubble.
We have devised the astounding capacity
to intervene in the very well-springs of life:
man can use this power for good, within the bounds of the moral law,
or he can succumb to the short-sighted pride
of a science that accepts no limits,
but tramples on the respect due to every human being.
Today as never before in the past,
humanity stands at a crossroads.
And once again, O Virgin Most Holy,
salvation lies fully and uniquely in Jesus, your Son.

ACT OF ENTRUSTMENT TO MARY
October 8, 2000

In looking at the Holy Family, you, Christian spouses, are prompted to ask yourselves about the tasks that Christ assigns to you in your wonderful and demanding vocation.

Do not children themselves in a way continually "examine" their parents? They do so not only with their frequent "why?"s but with their very faces, sometimes smiling, sometimes misty with sadness. It is as if a question were inscribed in their whole existence, a question that is expressed in the most varied ways, even in their whims, and that we could put into questions like these: Mama, papa, do you love me? Am I really a gift for you? Do you accept me for what I am? Do you always try to do what is really best for me?

These questions perhaps are asked more with their eyes than in words, but they hold parents to their great responsibility and are in some way an echo of God's voice for them.

SPEECH AT THE JUBILEE OF FAMILIES
October 14, 2000

Dear friends, you who are children and young people today will tomorrow form the first generation of adult Christians in the third millennium. What a great responsibility you have! You will be the leading players at the next Jubilee in 2025. You will then be grown-ups: you may have started a family of your own or have embraced the priestly life or been consecrated to a special mission in the Church at the service of God and neighbor.

And I, who have had the great satisfaction of leading the Church into the third millennium, look at you with my heart full of hope. In your eyes, in your tender faces, I can already glimpse the milestone of the next Jubilee. I look into the distance and pray for you. Dear young people, keep aloft and shining brightly the lamp of faith, which this evening I symbolically entrust to you and to your contemporaries in every corner of the world. With this light, illumine the paths of life; set the world ablaze with love!

SPEECH TO CHILDREN AT JUBILEE CLOSING
January 5, 2001

Sometimes when we look at the young, with the problems and weaknesses that characterize them in contemporary society, we tend to be pessimistic. The Jubilee of Young People, however, changed that, telling us that young people, whatever their possible ambiguities, have a profound longing for those genuine values that find their fullness in Christ. Is not Christ the secret of true freedom and profound joy of heart? Is not Christ the supreme friend and the teacher of all genuine friendship? If Christ is presented to young people as he really is, they experience him as an answer that is convincing and they can accept his message, even when it is demanding and bears the mark of the Cross. For this reason, in response to their enthusiasm, I did not hesitate to ask them to make a radical choice of faith and life and present them with a stupendous task: to become "morning watchmen" (cf. Is 21:11–12) at the dawn of the new millennium.

APOSTOLIC LETTER NOVO MILLENNIO INEUNTE, § 9
January 6, 2001

Jesus's cry on the Cross, dear brothers and sisters, is not the cry of anguish of a man without hope, but the prayer of the Son who offers his life to the Father in love, for the salvation of all. At the very moment when he identifies with our sin, "abandoned" by the Father, he "abandons" himself into the hands of the Father. His eyes remain fixed on the Father. Precisely because of the knowledge and experience of the Father, which he alone has, even at this moment of darkness he sees clearly the gravity of sin and suffers because of it. He alone, who sees the Father and rejoices fully in him, can understand completely what it means to resist the Father's love by sin. More than an experience of physical pain, his Passion is an agonizing suffering of the soul.

APOSTOLIC LETTER NOVO MILLENNIO INEUNTE, § 26
January 6, 2001

Yes, dear brothers and sisters, our Christian communities must become genuine "schools" of prayer, where the meeting with Christ is expressed not just in imploring help but also in thanksgiving, praise, adoration, contemplation, listening, and ardent devotion, until the heart truly "falls in love." Intense prayer, yes, but it does not distract us from our commitment to history: by opening our heart to the love of God, it also opens it to the love of our brothers and sisters, and makes us capable of shaping history according to God's plan.

APOSTOLIC LETTER NOVO MILLENNIO INEUNTE, § 33
January 6, 2001

You in particular, my sick friends, understand how paradoxical the Cross is, because you are allowed to feel the mystery of pain in your own flesh. When your strength fails because of a serious illness, projects you have long cherished in your heart are abandoned. In addition to physical suffering, there is often spiritual suffering due to a sense of loneliness that grips the individual. In contemporary society, a certain culture considers the sick person a troublesome hindrance, failing to recognize that he makes a valuable spiritual contribution to the community. It is necessary and urgent to rediscover the value of the Cross we share with Christ.

Working together, you must seek to provide increasing material and moral support to women in difficulty, victims of poverty and violence. Never forget that this important work is rooted in God's love and will bear fruit to the extent that your witness reveals his infinite love for every human person.

Feminine holiness, to which each one of you is called, is indispensable to the life of the Church. "The Second Vatican Council, confirming the teaching of the whole of tradition, recalled that in the hierarchy of holiness it is precisely the 'woman,' Mary of Nazareth, who is the 'figure' of the Church. She 'precedes' everyone on the path to holiness" (*Mulieris Dignitatem*, 27). Women who live in holiness are "a model of the 'sequela Christi,' an example of how the Bride must respond with love to the love of the Bridegroom" (ibid, 27).

Put out into the deep to go where? The answer is clear: to reach out to man, an unfathomable mystery; and to go to all people, a boundless ocean. This is possible in a missionary Church, which is able to speak to people and, especially, to touch the human heart, because the saving encounter with Christ occurs there, in that intimate and sacred place.

Dear friends, in my ministry I have never tired of meeting people; this is the goal of the pilgrimages and pastoral visits I continue to make. Even now as the years go by, I do not intend to stop, if this is God's will, because I am convinced that it is easier to proclaim Christ through personal contact with others.

SPEECH TO ROMAN YOUTH
April 5, 2001

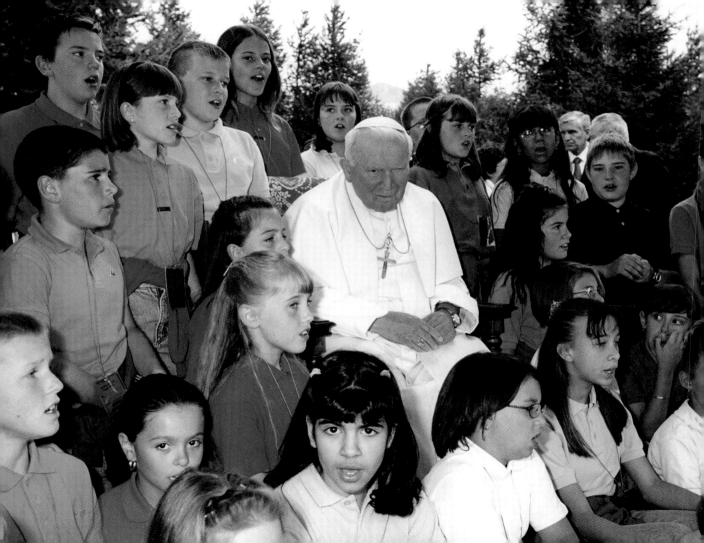

333

Proclaiming and bearing witness to the Gospel involves many difficulties. Yes, it is true: we live at a time when society is strongly influenced by models of life that give priority to possessions, pleasure, and appearances in a selfish sense. The missionary thrust of believers has to deal with this way of thinking and acting. But we must not be afraid, because Christ can change the human heart and is capable of working a "miraculous catch" when we least imagine.

SPEECH TO ROMAN YOUTH
April 5, 2001

Dear young people, you are going through a time of life filled with questions and uncertainties. Yet Christ is calling you and awakening in you a desire to make your life something magnificent and beautiful, a determination to pursue high ideals, a refusal to be satisfied with mediocrity, and the courage to make commitments, with patience and perseverance.

In order to be able to respond to this call, strive constantly to grow in closeness to the Lord of life. Remain faithfully in his presence through prayer, knowledge of the Scriptures, the celebration of the Eucharist, and the Sacrament of Reconciliation. In this way you will build yourselves up and strengthen what the apostle Paul calls "your inner self." An intimate relationship with the Lord is also the secret behind a fruitful life, a life grounded in what is essential for every human being: namely, dialogue with God, our Creator and our Savior. In this way, your life will not be superficial, but profoundly rooted in the spiritual, moral, and human values that sustain our whole being and our whole existence.

MEETING WITH YOUTH AT THE GREEK CATHOLIC CATHEDRAL, DAMASCUS, SYRIA
May 7, 2001

We have come to Assisi on a pilgrimage of peace. We are here, as representatives of different religions, to examine ourselves before God concerning our commitment to peace, to ask him for this gift, to bear witness to our shared longing for a world of greater justice and solidarity.

We wish to do our part in fending off the dark clouds of terrorism, hatred, armed conflict, which in these last few months have grown particularly ominous on humanity's horizon. For this reason we wish to listen to one another. We believe that this itself is already a sign of peace. In listening to one another there is already a reply to the disturbing questions that worry us. This already serves to scatter the shadows of suspicion and misunderstanding.

The shadows will not be dissipated with weapons; darkness is dispelled by sending out bright beams of light. A few days ago I reminded the diplomatic corps accredited to the Holy See that hatred can only be overcome through love.

SPEECH TO REPRESENTATIVES OF WORLD RELIGIONS, ASSISI, ITALY
January 24, 2002

I am grateful to the young men and women who have manifested to me their desire to respond to the call of the Lord, but at the same time have realized that it is not always easy to respond to him with an open and generous "yes."

Dear friends, I understand your difficulty. The numerous offers that you have to weigh in your mind that come from every side certainly do not make it any easier for you to discern the wonderful plan of life whose unifying center and driving force are Christ. Isn't it true that some of your peers seem to live for the moment, choosing what appears to be the easiest course?

Listen to me! If you do not give time to prayer nor accept the counsel of a spiritual guide, the confusion of the world can even succeed in drowning God's voice. As some have quickly observed, by satisfying our own immediate needs we lose the capacity to love in the name of Christ and become incapable of giving our lives for others as he has taught us. What should we do then?

SPEECH TO ROMAN YOUTH
March 21, 2002

What call will those on early morning watch choose to follow? To believe in Jesus is to accept what he says, even when it runs contrary to what others are saying. It means rejecting the lure of sin, however attractive it may be, in order to set out on the difficult path of the Gospel virtues.

Young people listening to me, answer the Lord with strong and generous hearts! He is counting on you. Never forget: Christ needs you to carry out his plan of salvation! Christ needs your youth and your generous enthusiasm to make his proclamation of joy resound in the new millennium. Answer his call by placing your lives at his service in your brothers and sisters! Trust Christ, because he trusts you.

The contemplation of Christ has an incomparable model in Mary. In a unique way the face of the Son belongs to Mary. It was in her womb that Christ was formed, receiving from her a human resemblance, which points to an even greater spiritual closeness. No one has ever devoted himself to the contemplation of the face of Christ as faithfully as Mary. The eyes of her heart already turned to him at the Annunciation, when she conceived him by the power of the Holy Spirit. In the months that followed she began to sense his presence and to picture his features. When at last she gave birth to him in Bethlehem, her eyes were able to gaze tenderly on the face of her Son, as she "wrapped him in swaddling cloths, and laid him in a manger" (Lk 2:7).

APOSTOLIC LETTER ROSARIUM VIRGINIS MARIAE, § 10
October 16, 2002

Thereafter Mary's gaze, ever filled with adoration and wonder, would never leave him. At times it would be a questioning look, as in the episode of the finding in the Temple: "Son, why have you done this to us?" (Lk 2:48); it would always be a penetrating gaze, one capable of deeply understanding Jesus, even to the point of perceiving his hidden feelings and anticipating his decisions, as at Cana (cf. Jn 2:5). At other times it would be a look of sorrow, especially beneath the Cross, where her vision would still be that of a mother giving birth, for Mary not only shared the Passion and Death of her Son, she also received the new son given to her in the beloved disciple. On the morning of Easter hers would be a gaze radiant with the joy of the Resurrection, and finally, on the day of Pentecost, a gaze afire with the outpouring of the Spirit.

APOSTOLIC LETTER ROSARIUM VIRGINIS MARIAE, § 10
October 16, 2002

Mary lived with her eyes fixed on Christ, treasuring his every word: "Mary kept all these things, reflecting on them in her heart" (Lk 2:19; cf. 2:51). The memories of Jesus, impressed upon her heart, were always with her, leading her to reflect on the various moments of her life at her Son's side. In a way those memories were to be the "rosary," which she recited uninterruptedly throughout her earthly life.

Even now, amid the joyful songs of the heavenly Jerusalem, the reasons for her thanksgiving and praise remain unchanged. They inspire her maternal concern for the pilgrim Church, in which she continues to relate her personal account of the Gospel. Mary constantly sets before the faithful the "mysteries" of her Son, with the desire that the contemplation of those mysteries will release all their saving power. In the recitation of the Rosary, the Christian community enters into contact with the memories and the contemplative gaze of Mary.

APOSTOLIC LETTER ROSARIUM VIRGINIS MARIAE, § 11
October 16, 2002

The Rosary is at the service of this ideal; it offers the "secret" that leads easily to a profound and inward knowledge of Christ. We might call it Mary's way. It is the way of the example of the Virgin of Nazareth, a woman of faith, of silence, of attentive listening. It is also the way of a Marian devotion inspired by knowledge of the inseparable bond between Christ and his Blessed Mother. The mysteries of Christ are also in some sense the mysteries of his Mother, even when they do not involve her directly, for she lives from him and through him. By making our own the words of the angel Gabriel and Saint Elizabeth contained in the Hail Mary, we find ourselves constantly drawn to seek out afresh in Mary, in her arms and in her heart, the "blessed fruit of her womb" (cf. Lk 1:42).

APOSTOLIC LETTER ROSARIUM VIRGINIS MARIAE, § 24
October 16, 2002

Beloved young men and young women! The slogan that will accompany you during this year of membership is: "Hands for everyone, everyone by the hand." Hands should not be used selfishly to hold on to material goods and practically cling to them. On the contrary, we must learn to keep our hands open to accept the love of God: hands always ready to receive and to transmit his love.

Live like this, and suggest this path to others your age as well!

SPEECH TO CATHOLIC ACTION YOUTH
December 20, 2002

Dear Christian families, proclaim joyfully to the whole world the wonderful treasure that you, as domestic churches, possess! Christian couples, in your communion of life and love, in your mutual self-giving and in your generous openness to children, become, in Christ, the light of the world. The Lord asks you daily to be like a lamp that does not remain hidden, but is "set on a lampstand, where it gives light to all in the house" (Mt 5:15).

Above all, be "good news" for the third millennium by remaining faithful to your vocation. Whether you were married recently or many years ago, the Sacrament of Matrimony continues to be your own special way of being disciples of Jesus, contributing to the spread of the Kingdom of God and growing in the holiness to which all Christians are called. As the Second Vatican Council noted, Christian couples, in the fulfillment of their marital and family responsibilities, "increasingly advance their own perfection and their mutual sanctification" (*Gaudium et Spes*, § 48).

TELEVISED MESSAGE TO WORLD MEETING OF FAMILIES IV, MANILA, PHILIPPINES
January 25, 2003

Firmly rooted in your history, look to the future with confidence and foresight. Charity impels you to open up ever new fields of action, to undertake new initiatives of human advancement and of evangelization in favor of the sick, the little ones, and the lowliest. This presupposes an intense spiritual life nourished by daily prayer, recourse to the sacraments, and serious personal ascetical effort. This is the soil in which you must sink the roots of your being and action.

As I urge you to persevere in your generous dedication, I assure you of my constant prayer to the Virgin of Nazareth, whom I would like to contemplate with you as, prompted by the Spirit, she pays a visit to her elderly cousin Elizabeth. May the Blessed Virgin, Our Lady of the Visitation, sustain you so that you may witness to the love of God who is ready to embrace and heal the human being and asks nothing in return.

MESSAGE TO UNITALSI (NATIONAL ITALIAN UNION FOR TRANSPORTING
THE SICK TO LOURDES AND INTERNATIONAL SHRINES)
February 26, 2003

"'Behold, your mother!' And from that hour," the Gospel continues, "the disciple took her into his home" (Jn 19:27).

Welcoming Mary into their home, into their life, is the privilege of every one of the faithful. This is especially true in difficult moments, such as those that you young people also have to live through at times in this period of your life.

Today I want to entrust you to Mary. Dear friends, and I tell you from experience, open the doors of your life to her! Do not be afraid to open wide the doors of your hearts to Christ through the One who wants to bring you to him, so that you may be saved from sin and death! She will help you to listen to his voice and say yes to every plan that God conceives for you, for your good and for that of all humanity.

The Church draws her life from the Eucharist. This truth does not simply express a daily experience of faith, but recapitulates the heart of the mystery of the Church. In a variety of ways she joyfully experiences the constant fulfillment of the promise: "Behold, I am with you always, until the end of the age" (Mt 28:20), but in the Holy Eucharist, through the changing of bread and wine into the body and blood of the Lord, she rejoices in this presence with unique intensity. Ever since Pentecost, when the Church, the People of the New Covenant, began her pilgrim journey toward her heavenly homeland, the Divine Sacrament has continued to mark the passing of her days, filling them with confident hope.

ENCYCLICAL ECCLESIA DE EUCARISTIA, § 1
April 17, 2003

There is a profound analogy between the "Fiat" that Mary said in reply to the angel and the "Amen" that every believer says when receiving the body of the Lord.

"Blessed are you who believed" (Lk 1:45). Mary also anticipated, in the mystery of the incarnation, the Church's Eucharistic faith. When, at the Visitation, she bore in her womb the Word made flesh, she became in some way a "tabernacle" — the first tabernacle in history — in which the Son of God, still invisible to our human gaze, allowed himself to be adored by Elizabeth, radiating his light as it were through the eyes and the voice of Mary. And is not the enraptured gaze of Mary as she contemplated the face of the newborn Christ and cradled him in her arms that unparalleled model of love that should inspire us every time we receive Eucharistic communion?

ENCYCLICAL ECCLESIA DE EUCARISTIA, § 55
April 17, 2003

When the body of Jesus is taken down from the Cross and laid in his Mother's arms, in our mind's eye we glimpse again the moment when Mary accepted the message brought by the angel Gabriel.

In the mystery of the redemption, grace—the gift of God himself—is interwoven with a "price" paid by the human heart. In this mystery we are enriched by a gift from on high (Jas 1:17) and at the same time "bought" by the ransom paid by the Son of God (cf. 1 Cor 6:20, 7:23; Acts 20:28). And Mary, who more than anyone was enriched by gifts, pays all the more. With her heart. Inseparable from this mystery is the extraordinary promise spoken of by Simeon during the Presentation of Jesus in the Temple: "(And you yourself a sword will pierce) so that the thoughts of many hearts may be revealed" (Lk 2:35).

This promise has also been fulfilled. How many human hearts bleed for the heart of this Mother who has paid so dearly!

Once again Jesus lies in her arms, as he did in the stable in Bethlehem (cf. Lk 2:16), during the flight into Egypt (cf. Mt 2:14), and at Nazareth (cf. Lk 2:39–40). *Pietà.*

MEDITATION AT THE THIRTEENTH STATION OF THE CROSS AT THE COLOSSEUM, ROME, ITALY
April 18, 2003

Mary, in addition to being our Mother who is close, discreet, and understanding, is the best teacher for achieving knowledge of the truth through contemplation. The drama of contemporary culture is the lack of interiority, the absence of contemplation. Without interiority, culture has no content; it is like a body that has not yet found its soul.

Dear young people, I invite you to be part of the "School of the Virgin Mary." She is the incomparable model of contemplation and wonderful example of fruitful, joyful, and enriching interiority. She will teach you never to separate action from contemplation, so as to contribute to making a great dream come true: the birth of the new Europe in the spirit.

SPEECH TO YOUTH, MADRID, SPAIN
May 3, 2003

On receiving the Nobel Prize for Peace, venerable Mother Teresa of Kolkata, whom you consider the spiritual president of the pro-life movements in the world, had the courage to say to the leaders of political communities: "If we let a mother kill the fruit of her womb, what is left to us? It is the principle of abortion that endangers peace in the world."

It is true! There can be no true peace without respect for life, especially if it is innocent and defenseless, as is that of the unborn child. Elementary coherence requires those who seek peace to safeguard life. No pro-peace activity can be effective unless attacks on life at all its stages, from conception until natural death, are as energetically opposed. Thus, your movement is not only a Pro-Life Movement but also an authentic peace movement, precisely because of your constant effort to protect life.

SPEECH TO THE ITALIAN PRO-LIFE MOVEMENT
May 22, 2003

Before me now I see the countless meetings I have had and all those who took part in them. Once again I would like to embrace them all, to tell them all of the love and prayers of the Pope, once again to invite them all to "open wide the doors to Christ"!

Dear brothers and sisters who are gathered here, I would like to say "thank you" to you. Your work at various levels and in various capacities has enabled the Pope to go to meet the men and women of our time in the places where they live. And you have helped him in his ministry as an itinerant missionary, eager to proclaim the words of salvation to all with the deep conviction that God wants "everyone to be saved and to come to knowledge of the truth" (1 Tm 2:4).

SPEECH TO THE PARTICIPANTS IN HIS ONE-HUNDREDTH APOSTOLIC JOURNEY
June 12, 2003

In your hearts and on your lips, God places three little words that are so important in the Bible: "Here I am." They were spoken by the Son of God when he came into the world, and his whole life was his constant prompt response of "here I am" to the heavenly Father.

"Here I am" was the Virgin Mary's response to the Angel of the Annunciation, who brought her God's announcement. With it, our Lady humbly accepted the mission of becoming Mother of Jesus and, hence, Mother of the Church.

"Here I am," you must learn to answer too, dear little missionaries, asking Jesus and Mary to help you. If you generously obey God's will, you will be able to experience the joy felt by so many missionary saints down the centuries who spent their lives for the Gospel.

SPEECH TO CHILDREN OF THE PONTIFICAL SOCIETY OF THE MISSIONARY CHILDHOOD
June 14, 2003

A "Missionary of Charity: this is what Mother Teresa was in name and in fact."
Today with deep feeling I repeat these words that I spoke the day after her death.

The Lord made this simple woman who came from one of Europe's poorest
regions a chosen instrument to proclaim the Gospel to the entire world, not by
preaching but by daily acts of love toward the poorest of the poor. A missionary
with the most universal language: the language of love that knows no bounds
or exclusion and has no preferences other than for the most forsaken.

A Missionary of Charity. A missionary of God who is love, who has a special
preference for the least and the humble, who bends over the human being
wounded in body and spirit and pours "the oil of consolation and the wine
of hope" upon the wounds. God did this in the person of his Son made man,
Jesus Christ, the Good Samaritan of humanity. He continues to do this in the
Church, especially through the saints of charity in whose ranks Mother Teresa
shines in a special way.

SPEECH TO PILGRIMS GATHERED FOR THE BEATIFICATION OF MOTHER TERESA OF KOLKATA
October 20, 2003

"Imitate what you will celebrate." A priest's pastoral service consists of a variety of actions of which, as the Council says, the Eucharist is the source and summit. Whatever its form, the invitation to imitate their deepest meaning is always timely and right. If a priest celebrates baptism — the sacrament of justification — is it not also his duty to be a witness of the justifying grace in his every action? If he prepares young people for the sacrament of Confirmation, which enables them to participate in the prophetic mission of the Church, should not he himself first be a faithful Gospel messenger? Thus, whenever he teaches, blesses marriages, accompanies the sick and prepares them for death, whenever he meets families — he himself must always witness first to the content of his service.

How different today's young people are from those of twenty years ago! How different is the cultural and social context in which we live! But Christ, no, he has not changed! He is the Redeemer of man yesterday, today, and forever!

The Pope is with you! Believe in Jesus, contemplate his Face, the Face of the crucified and risen Lord! That Face which so many long to see, but which is often veiled by our lack of enthusiasm for the Gospel and by our sin!

O beloved Jesus, reveal to us your Face of light and forgiveness! Look at us, renew us, send us out!

Too many young people are waiting for you, and if they do not see you, they will not be able to live their vocation, they will not be able to live life for you and with you, to renew the world beneath your gaze, which is turned to the Father and at the same time to our poor humanity.

SPEECH TO ROMAN YOUTH
April 1, 2004

I too was twenty, like you. I enjoyed sports, skiing, acting. I studied and I worked. I had desires and worries. In those years, now so long ago, when my native land was wounded by war and then by the totalitarian regime, I sought the meaning to give to my life. I found it in following the Lord Jesus.

Dear young woman, dear young man, youth is the period in which you wonder what to do with your life, how to contribute to making the world a little better, how to encourage justice and build peace.

If you are able to open your hearts and minds with availability, you will discover "your vocation"; in other words, the plan that God, in his love, has devised for you from eternity.

SPEECH TO SWISS CATHOLIC YOUTH, BERN, SWITZERLAND
June 5, 2004

Faithfully pursuing the path of our Redeemer from the poverty of the crib to his abandonment on the Cross, we can better understand the mystery of his love that redeems humanity. The Child, laid by Mary in the manger, is the man-God we shall see nailed to the Cross. The same Redeemer is present in the sacrament of the Eucharist. In the stable at Bethlehem he allowed himself to be worshipped under the humble outward appearances of a newborn baby, by Mary, by Joseph, and by the shepherds; in the consecrated Host we adore him sacramentally present in his body, blood, soul, and godhead, and he offers himself to us as the food of eternal life. The Mass then becomes a truly loving encounter with the One who gave himself wholly for us. Do not hesitate, my dear young friends, to respond to him when he invites you "to the wedding feast of the Lamb" (Rev 19:9). Listen to him, prepare yourselves properly, and draw close to the Sacrament of the Altar.

"Stay with us, Lord, for it is almost evening" (Lk 24:29). This was the insistent invitation that the two disciples journeying to Emmaus on the evening of the day of the Resurrection addressed to the Wayfarer who had accompanied them on their journey. . . . Amid the shadows of the passing day and the darkness that clouded their spirit, the Wayfarer brought a ray of light that rekindled their hope and led their hearts to yearn for the fullness of light. "Stay with us," they pleaded. And he agreed. Soon afterward, Jesus's face would disappear, yet the Master would "stay" with them, hidden in the "breaking of the bread," which had opened their eyes to recognize him.

Amid our questions and difficulties, and even our bitter disappointments, the divine Wayfarer continues to walk at our side, opening to us the Scriptures and leading us to a deeper understanding of the mysteries of God. When we meet him fully, we will pass from the light of the Word to the light streaming from the "bread of life," the supreme fulfillment of his promise to "be with us always, to the end of the age."

APOSTOLIC LETTER MANE NOBISCUM DOMINE, §§ 1–2
October 7, 2004

When the disciples on the way to Emmaus asked Jesus to stay "with" them, he responded by giving them a much greater gift: through the Sacrament of the Eucharist, he found a way to stay "in" them. Receiving the Eucharist means entering into a profound communion with Jesus. "Abide in me, and I in you" (Jn 15:4). This relationship of profound and mutual "abiding" enables us to have a certain foretaste of heaven on Earth. Is this not the greatest of human yearnings? Is this not what God had in mind when he brought about in history his plan of salvation? God has placed in human hearts a "hunger" for his word, a hunger that will be satisfied only by full union with him. Eucharistic communion was given so that we might be "sated" with God here on Earth, in expectation of our complete fulfillment in heaven.

APOSTOLIC LETTER MANE NOBISCUM DOMINE, § 19
October 7, 2004

Immaculate Virgin!
Once again we are here to honor you, at the foot of this column
from which you lovingly watch over Rome and the whole world. . . .

Immaculate Virgin!
Your spotless spiritual beauty is for us a living source of confidence and hope.
To have you as Mother, Holy Virgin,
reassures us on the path of life as a pledge of eternal salvation.
Because of this, O Mary,
we have recourse to you with confidence.
Help us to build a world where human life is always cherished and defended,
every form of violence banished, the peace of all tenaciously sought.

TRIBUTE TO THE STATUE OF THE IMMACULATE CONCEPTION OF THE BLESSED VIRGIN MARY,
PIAZZA DI SPAGNA, ROME, ITALY
December 8, 2004

In today's Gospel, Jesus proclaims, "Blessed are the peacemakers" (Mt 5:9). These little ones can also be peacemakers! They too must train themselves in dialogue and must learn to "conquer evil with good" (Rom 12:21), as I recalled for everyone in the recent message for the World Day of Peace. It is necessary to defeat injustice with justice, falsehood with truth, vengeance with forgiveness, hate with love.

This lifestyle is not improvised but requires education, beginning in infancy. This education comes from wise teachings and above all from sound models in the family, in school, and in every part of society. Parishes, oratories, associations, movements, and ecclesial groups must more and more become privileged places of this pedagogy of peace and love, where growing together is learned.

Once again, dear brothers and sisters, I address you from the Agostino Gemelli Polyclinic. I warmly thank you and feel you all close to me in spirit. I think of you, individuals and groups who are gathered today in Saint Peter's Square, and all those from all over the world who are concerned about me. I ask that you continue to assist me, especially with your prayers.

The penitential season of Lent that we are living helps us to understand better the value of suffering, which in one way or another touches us all. It is in looking at Christ and following him with patient trust that we are able to understand how every human form of suffering contains a divine promise of salvation and joy. I desire that this message of comfort and hope reaches everyone, especially those who are going through difficult moments and those who suffer in body and in spirit.

To Mary, Mother of the Church, I once again entrust myself: Totus tuus! May she help us to fulfill God's will in every moment of life.

ANGELUS
February 27, 2005

In today's Gospel, as he cures the man born blind, Christ presents himself as "the light of the world" (Jn 9:5). He came to open human eyes to the light of faith. Yes, dear friends, faith is the light that guides us on our way through life, it is the flame that comforts us in difficult times.

When a child is born we say that the baby "comes into the light." For believers, who are born to supernatural life through baptism, Lent is a favorable time to "come into the light," that is, to be reborn in the Spirit, renewing the grace and commitment of baptism.

May Mary Most Holy help us to obtain from Christ the gift of an ever stronger and clearer faith, so that we may be consistent and courageous witnesses of his Gospel.

ANGELUS
March 6, 2005

"Adoro Te devote, latens Deitas!" Let us raise our eyes to Jesus in the Eucharist; let us contemplate him and repeat to him together these words written by Saint Thomas Aquinas that express all our faith and love: "Devoutly I adore you, hidden Deity, under these appearances concealed."

In an epoch marked by hatred, selfishness, the desire for false happiness, by the decadence of customs, the absence of father and mother figures, instability in numerous young families, and by widespread frailty and hardship to which many young people fall prey, we look to you, Jesus in the Eucharist, with renewed hope. In spite of our sins we trust in your divine Mercy. We repeat to you, together with the disciples of Emmaus, "Mane nobiscum Domine!"—"Stay with us, Lord!"

MESSAGE TO YOUTH AT EUCHARISTIC ADORATION IN SAINT JOHN LATERAN, ROME, ITALY
March 15, 2005

The adoration of the Cross directs us to a commitment that we cannot shirk: the mission that Saint Paul expressed in these words: "in my flesh I am filling up what is lacking in the afflictions of Christ on behalf of his body, which is the Church" (Col 1:24). I also offer my sufferings so that God's plan may be completed and his Word spread among the peoples. I, in turn, am close to all who are tried by suffering at this time. I pray for each one of them.

On this memorable day of Christ's crucifixion, I look at the Cross with you in adoration, repeating the words of the liturgy: "O crux, ave spes unica!"— Hail, O Cross, our only hope, give us patience and courage and obtain peace for the world!

MESSAGE TO PARTICIPANTS IN THE WAY OF THE CROSS AT THE COLOSSEUM, ROME, ITALY
March 25, 2005

Editor's Note: listed below are the captions only for reproductions of artworks and photographs depicting historical events. Each number refers to the meditation.

Photography Credits:

The photographs are indicated by the number of corresponding meditation.

Cover image: © Bernard Bisson/Sygma/Corbis

© *Osservatore Romano*: 10, 16, 23, 29, 33, 40, 46, 64, 85, 97, 105, 133, 134, 137, 140, 147, 151, 160, 175, 183, 186, 191, 200, 201, 204, 207, 210, 211, 218, 219, 225, 229, 240, 253, 259, 268, 285, 297, 303, 318, 319, 321, 332, 334, 339, 342, 354, 364

© Chirulli/CONTRASTO: 3
© Tomki Nemec/Anzenberger/CONTRASTO: 58
© Tania A3/CONTRASTO: 70
© Album – Oronoz/Album/CONTRASTO: 93
© Ralf Tooten/ laif /CONTRASTO: 351

© Vittoriano Rastelli/CORBIS: 1, 20, 69

© Archivio Farabola: 67, 114, 163, 172, 241, 246, 365

© RCS Periodici: 18, 31, 42, 44, 120, 157, 182, 323, 337, 343, 346, 353, 359

© Lorenzo Casella: 327, 336, 356

© Giuseppe Cirasino: 47, 51, 59, 73, 92, 226, 257, 302

© Sara Cremaschi: 294

© Sergio Daniotti: 54, 79, 113, 117, 313

© Franco Sartori: 28, 41, 89, 100, 258, 280, 292, 307, 333

© Davide Vincenti: 27, 273, 309

All other images © Archivio Shutterstock

Every effort has been made to identify all images in this book. Any inaccuracies brought to the editor's attention will be corrected for future editions.